Secret

Strategies

That

Reveal

the Real

Him

50 Ways

to Read
Your Lover

A LARK PRODUCTION

Todd Lyon

A FIRESIDE BOOK
PUBLISHED BY SIMON & SCHUSTER
NEW YORK LONDON TORONTO SYDNEY SINGAPORE

FIRESIDE
Rockefeller Center
1230 Avenue of the Americas
New York, NY 10020

For information about special discounts for bulk purchases,
please contact Simon & Schuster Special Sales:
1-800-456-6798 or business@simonandschuster.com

Designed by ELINA D. NUDELMAN

Manufactured in the United States of America

10   9   8   7   6   5   4   3   2   1

Library of Congress Cataloging-in-Publication Data

Lyon, Todd.
    50 ways to read your lover : secret strategies that
reveal the real him / Todd Lyon.
        p.   cm.
    "A Lark production."
    1. Mate selection—Miscellanea.   2. Man-woman
relationships—Miscellanea.   3. Men—Psychology—
Miscellanea.   I. Title: Fifty ways to read your lover.
II. Title.
HQ801.L96   2003
646.7'7—dc21   2002029755

ISBN 0-7432-2956-8

Acknowledgments

The idea for this book sprang from the inventive and slightly boy-crazy mind of my friend and colleague Karen Watts, with a significant assist from her comrades at Lark Productions.

I came rushing in to make Karen's metaphysical dream a reality, but my work could not have been done (on time, anyway) without the help of Hayward Gatling, who spent approximately 28 days and nights researching subjects that ranged from body language to tea leaves—which was quite a stretch for a guy whose usual expertise is in construction, combustion engines, and ham. Support also poured in from my wonderful family and friends, with gold stars going to Barbara Lyon and Sandra Shea for their insightful contributions.

A majority of the 50 ways presented in this book are based on profound practices that are associated with spiritual, religious, or sacred belief systems. Due to practical constraints, I've had to abbreviate and/or simplify these mystical arts to a degree that, in some cases, may seem irreverent. But I am not irreverent. Quite the contrary. My sincerest hope is for the true spirit of these ancient teachings to come through and for readers to be inspired to pursue deeper studies of the systems that speak to them.

My gratitude goes out to those legions of practitioners — be they shamans, psychics, healers, readers, empaths, channelers, or fortune-tellers — who have kept the old magic alive throughout centuries of change. Thanks, too, to the visionary physicians and psychologists who work to create a balance between science and the spirit.

I bow to them, and beg their approval, forgiveness, understanding, and good chi.

Contents

50 Ways

to Read
Your Lover

Introduction

*Dear wonderful, passionate, fragile, resilient,
romantic, curious, desirable, brilliant Goddess of the
Earth and Sky:*

*I know why you're reading this book. It's because
you're consumed by love. You probably remember a
time when you followed your own voice and did what
you thought was right for you, without question.
Now, your inner signals are scrambled. You're
overwhelmed with feelings of ecstasy, doubt, and
longing, and you've found that these emotions are far
more compelling than prim little intellectual
mechanisms such as logic and rational thinking.*

*Don't be ashamed. Love is a powerful force.
Tornadoes and hurricanes may destroy your house
and toss your car into a tree, but love gets into your
bloodstream. It messes with your very chemistry and
can lead you into flirtation, sex, marriage, and/or
betrayal of your best friend—all of which are
potentially more damaging than house-wrecking or
car-flinging.*

*When the heart eclipses the mind, a girl's got to
reach out. She's got to tap into ancient systems of*

wisdom and glean advice from seasoned sorcerers and prognosticators who know what's up and what's down.

So, you've come to the right place. The book you hold in your hand condenses a whole universe of romantic insight into one intense yet easy-to-use volume. Here is a collection of tools to help you learn the secrets of his soul; compare compatibility factors; understand hidden meanings behind his body language, his handshake, his eyes, his driving style; plus quizzes and games that the two of you can take together. He'll think they're fun. You'll use them for their intended purpose: as emotional divining rods.

The wilderness of love shouldn't be navigated without a guidebook. This one is full of maps, and it is my sincerest hope that one, twelve, twenty-seven, or all fifty of them will lead you to your heart's truest destination.

Love forever,
Todd Lyon

A Spy in the House of Love

In the early throes of love, every woman is a private investigator. Including you.

Don't deny it. I've been there. I know.

Whether you're sizing up a hunky stranger or testing the worthiness of your new or possible new boyfriend, your antennae are fully extended, straining to pick up clues that may affect your romantic future. But you don't want to get caught, right? You don't want to seem anxious. You especially don't want to seem needy, nosy, aggressive, or — God forbid — desperate.

Relax. Chapter One is at your rescue. Its exercises can supply you with tons of valuable insights about the guy, without his suspecting a thing. Most are based on your own private observations (face reading, pupil reactions, body language), while some require basic information to work with (handwriting analysis, numerology, sleep positions).

You needn't say a word to anyone. Learn what you can, smile a private smile, and remember that information is power.

CHINESE FACE READING (SIANG MIEN)

That certain face might seem nothing but wonderful to you . . . but what does it mean to practitioners of siang mien, the ancient Chinese art of face reading?

The seven basic facial types in the following section have been used for centuries to reveal the kind of character that lies behind a man's visage (yes, it also works for women). The first thing you need to do is examine the relative visual measurements of your subject's face. (It helps to have a photograph in hand that's been taken straight-on; in fact, driver's license photos and passport photos are useful for this exercise.) Take note of:

HEIGHT: The height of the forehead region, from the hairline to the top of the eyebrows (in the case of baldness, consider the boundaries of the former hairline); the distance between the eyebrows and the tip of the nose (encompassing the eye and cheek region); and the distance between the tip of the nose to the bottom of the chin (the length of the jaw area).

WIDTH: The width of the forehead (the distance between the temples); the width of the cheeks (the distance between the protrusions of the cheekbones); and the width of the jawbone midway between its widest and narrowest point.

The Seven Faces and What They Represent

1. **SQUARE:** The face is as tall as it is wide; the forehead, cheeks, and jaw area are about the same width.

    Character: "Iron." Hard and tough, with strong leadership qualities; decisive, dedicated, and stable.

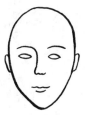

2. **TAPERED SQUARE:** The height and width of the face are about the same, but each of the three widths tapers toward the base.

Character: "Bucket." Brilliant, generous, and creative, with inner strength; moods can fluctuate between ecstatic, gloomy, and calm.

3. **PYRAMID:** The forehead and cheeks are narrower than the jaw.

Character: "Earth." Practical, stubborn, resilient, hard working, persistent, slow and determined.

4. **INVERTED PYRAMID:** The forehead is wide, the cheekbones are prominent, and the chin is pointed and triangular.

Character: "Fire." Quick, bright, sensitive, sexual, passionate, entertaining, powerful, and vivacious.

5. **WIDE:** The face is wider than it is long, and the three widths are about equal.

   Character: "Wall." Guarded, solid, protective, strong, lives in the moment; can be uncommunicative or reactionary.

6. **DIAMOND:** The width of the cheeks is greater than those of the forehead and jaw.

   Character: "Jade." Mystical, elegant, talented, sharp, durable, active, caring; can be possessive.

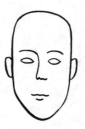

7. **LONG:** The face is longer than it is wide, and the three widths are about equal.

   Character: "Tree." Courageous, independent, mature, nurturing, assertive; prone to aggressiveness or abruptness.

WESTERN-STYLE FACE READING

In the United States, face reading is a casual affair. Compared to the discipline of siang mien, our version could barely be called a system. Here's a quickie overview anyway; it deals strictly with the five basic contours of the face.

Face Shapes

- **SQUARE:** Belongs to a stable person who is firm and energetic, yet possibly inflexible and stubborn, too.

- **ANGULAR:** Indicates an ambitious, clever character who may also be — but hopefully isn't — selfish and greedy.

- **POINTED:** This is the face of a sophisticated, inspired person who's always on the go. Watch out for dishonest or hypocritical tendencies.

- **ROUNDED:** At best, the owner of this face is gentle, jovial, and frank. At worst, he is indecisive and slow.

- **SOFT:** The sign of a sweet, sensuous, and mild-mannered individual who no doubt resists his capacity for dullness, apathy, and laziness.

PUPIL REACTIONS

The fastest way to a man's heart is not through his stomach. It's through his eyes. And guess what? That's the fastest way for him to reach your heart, too.

Here's the deal: When a man is attracted to a woman, his pupils automatically dilate — that is, the black circles in the center of his eyes grow larger. The same thing happens to women when they're attracted to men. What's cool about this phenomenon is we, as human animals, are hardwired to believe that people with large pupils are more desirable than those with tiny pupils. So by looking deeply into the eyes of men whom we want/crave/ love, we can not only take a reading of their pupil reactions but also send them a sexy, irresistible, dilated gaze.

So stare. Stare with intensity. Find out what you need to know, and send a message that can't be missed.

Disclaimer #1: If you're in a brightly illuminated environment — say, a ski slope on a sunny day — both of you will have small pupils, no matter what.

Disclaimer #2: If you're in a dimly lit environment — say, a dark and smoky martini bar — both of you will have dilated pupils, no matter what.

TYPE A OR TYPE B?

It's great to be ambitious, inspired, and driven to succeed. These are admirable qualities in any man, whether he is an entrepreneur, a grave digger, a student, an athlete, an executive, or a person recovering from an injury.

It's also great to be laid-back and able to roll with the punches while fully enjoying the pleasures of life.

Best of all is a man who is a robust and balanced combination of the two.

The overview below will help you to figure out if your love interest is a high-strung achiever (type A), a low-key pleasure puppy (type B), or a little of both.

How to Spot a Type A Personality

- Because A types are always in a hurry, they have few qualms about displaying their impatience with any form of slowness, delays, or glitches.
- Type A's focus on results at any cost; not only are they fast talking and fast thinking, they can also be abrupt and rude.
- Competition is every A man's middle name. He strives to outdo even those who are inexperienced

or less skilled, needing to exhibit their expertise on whatever subject is being discussed.

- A types also thrive on multitasking. You can find them talking on the phone while driving, networking at weddings and funerals, and listening to stock reports while showering.

- Your A amour is in perpetual motion; while sitting, he may jiggle his knees, tap his pen, ruffle through paperwork, or all three.

Perhaps you've seen your guy exhibit more than a few of these behaviors. You're probably wondering, What's so bad about being on the fast track? Here's what's so bad:

1. Type A people judge their own worth in units of measurable success. It's all about numbers: their net income, the profits they stand to earn on a deal, the cost of their car, the pedigrees of their possessions, how much their client dropped on dinner, how close they rubbed elbows with the rich and famous . . . this is what matters to them.

2. The pursuit of material goals can cause them to be blind, deaf, and numb to the beauty of the world around them. Instead of stopping to smell the flowers, they stop and read the price tags.

3. They are so committed to their goals that love and romance is forced into the background. When type A's do manage to hook up, the relationship is disposable. Their dreams of grandeur are not.

4. Type A behavior is sustained by constant anxiety and tension. Even when this person relaxes (or collapses), he feels guilty and nervous about what isn't getting done.

5. The type A individual is prone to heart attacks and other unpleasant side effects. Studies show that As are four times more likely to develop coronary heart disease than type Bs.

How to Spot a Type B Personality

- Type B people are more tortoise than hare. Though they might have an overall career plan, they take the journey one step at a time and dedicate themselves to the task at hand.
- They don't rush jobs. Nor do they waste time on procrastination or mad haste that ultimately causes delays.
- When presented with a challenge, Mr. B doesn't believe that the solution rests exclusively on his shoulders. He shares the responsibility — and the stress — via delegation or other group efforts.

- B types consider financial prosperity to be only one portion of their overall success rating. Their inner pie charts may be divided equally between a happy family life, ongoing spiritual development, fun vacations, satisfying hobbies, profound love relationships, a healthy body, a good sex life, and a decent paycheck.
- B men have fewer health problems than A types. In true tortoise fashion, they enjoy longer lives and reach their goals with very little suffering, anxiety, hysteria, shame, guilt, punishment, ego problems, or self-deprivation.

Of course, there are negative aspects to being a B man. This comes as no surprise, does it? Read on:

1. Some B types are relaxed to a fault. These guys can fall into the category of slacker, loser, load, lazy bum, freeloader, or other unattractive title. If you can't stand the idea of a man who lies on the sofa watching television all day, steer clear of guys who are all B and no A.

2. B boys are sensual creatures and love to feel good. Sometimes their pursuit of pleasant sensations goes too far, and in extreme cases it can lead to substance abuse.

3. Many Bs are good providers when it comes to companionship, communication, and emotional support. They're not necessarily great, however, when it comes to providing financial support. If material prosperity is essential to your overall sense of security and well-being, stick with A types.

4. Classic B types don't have take-charge personalities. If you're independent and powerful, his passivity may be an asset to your relationship. But if you want a man who takes the lead now and then, the B-type guy could cause you much frustration and could very well turn you into a full-time nag.

A Plus B Equals . . .

The best of both worlds. When shopping for a mate, look for a guy who is steady and grounded (a basic B type) but who can go into overdrive and pull out type A behaviors whenever situations call for it.

A MEETING OF THE BODY AND MIND

Every individual's body is unique. We each have our own blood type, skeletal structure, palm print, voice print, dental records, and DNA. In fact, the entire field of forensics wouldn't exist if each of us weren't one of a kind.

From a distance, however, many humans look alike, which is probably what prompted psychologist William H. Sheldon in the early 1940s to identify and name three basic body types: endomorphic, mesomorphic, and ectomorphic. Taking it one step further, Dr. Sheldon suggested that certain personality traits were associated with each physical archetype.

Granted, his studies showed that very few people — if any — matched the archetypes to a T. But his observations have stood the test of time, and his terminology still pops up in discussions between smart people. For you, the body-based types provide an interesting jumping-off point when you want to sketch a broad psychological profile of someone you're watching.

Endomorph

With a shape that's rounded and soft, the classic endomorph is overweight and stores much of his excess fat in the abdomen area. The legs are often shorter than the torso; the muscles are underdeveloped; and the skin is smooth.

Personality-wise, endomorphs tend to be amiable, warm, and generous. They are tolerant, sociable, slow to anger, and even-tempered. As realists, their actions are deliberate and practical, yet carried out in a relaxed and unhurried way.

Endomorphs need confirmation of the tangible world and often connect with it through immediate sensations, such as eating and physical affection. This type craves comfort and can easily fall into habitual behavior.

Mesomorph

Usually of medium height with well-developed shoulders, the archetypal mesomorph has an angular or rectangular-shaped body, with thick skin, dense muscle mass, and upright posture.

Mesomorphs are action-oriented, dynamic, adventurous, and self-assertive. They're natural leaders and enjoy taking on challenges, especially those that require physical exertion. Not prone to introspection, mesomorphs are usually set in their ways and rely on their courage and energy to get what they want.

Many mesomorphs strive for power and dominance. They are competitive by nature and, in extreme instances, could display aggressive behavior and an indifference to others' needs.

Ectomorph

The archetypal ectomorph is tall and thin, with long legs and a narrow torso. The shoulders might be stooped and the chest might be flat, but the head is usually quite large. Ectomorphs tend to have delicate or even fragile builds, with a minimum amount of visible muscle.

The ectomorph is the most mentally intense and physically sensitive of the three types. Cerebral, attentive, and artistic, ectomorphs are introverted and prefer privacy and solitude to social interaction. They're often inhibited about their bodies and their emotions, keeping both to themselves.

Relaxation and deep sleep can elude the ectomorph due to the nervous energy that courses through his system. It's especially difficult for this type to find a comfortable balance between the body and the mind.

KNOW YOUR DOSHAS

Vata. Pitta. Kapha. Do these words make you think of college sororities? If so, then you've probably never heard of Ayurvedic medicine, a sacred, holistic life science that has been practiced in India for more than 5,000 years.

The Ayurvedic system centers around three essential body/mind/spirit types, known as doshas. Each dosha has specific characteristics, and most people can identify themselves as being similar in type to at least one of the three. Optimum health and well-being is achieved when the doshas are harmoniously balanced. It is the Ayurvedic physician's job to create that balance, which is achieved by dietary changes or other lifestyle adjustments.

Vata, pitta, and kapha are the three doshas of Ayurveda. By studying the descriptions below, you can pinpoint your man's dosha and learn a bit about what makes him tick. At the same time, you can look at your loved one through a filter of 5,000 years of wisdom and healing.

Vata

Physically, the vata type is slender and light, with narrow hips and shoulders. Lively, energetic, and self-confident, he has swift movements and a fast walk. It's easy for him to learn new things, but he tends to forget them just as quickly. He can be imaginative, excitable, and unpredictable; he is better at starting things than finishing them.

When his dosha is out of balance, the body surges with nervous energy, and Mr. Vata may become anxious, forgetful, distracted, and easily exhausted. Though he's usually a light but sound sleeper, an imbalance can lead to insomnia and a heightened sensitivity to noise.

Pitta

The pitta type is a well-proportioned person of medium build (or thereabouts). He tends to have fair yet ruddy skin, precise speech patterns, sudden hunger pangs, a determined walk, and an aversion to direct sunlight. Personality-wise, he is warm, friendly, and charismatic; he has a curious mind, a love of challenges, and an enterprising nature.

When the pitta dosha is out of balance, he can turn irritable, severely critical, combative, and jealous. Under pressure, he gets stressed out and short-tempered, and may become hyperconscious of time and fixated on completing tasks.

Kapha

The kapha man has a powerful, soft-edged body with wide shoulders and thick hair. Steady and methodical, he speaks slowly and learns slowly but has great retention and stamina. By nature he is relaxed, easygoing, tolerant, steady, and affectionate. He also tends to hang on to everything, including possessions, money, and weight.

When the kapha dosha is out of balance, the result could be lethargy, depression, boredom, weight gain, stubbornness, procrastination, greed, and excessive sleeping.

BODY LANGUAGE

One delightfully sneaky way to get to know the "real him" is to observe and analyze his body language. This method is most accurate when used in business settings, although it can also work in social situations. Be aware that each position relates to the circumstances at hand and shouldn't be used to judge his overall character—just his reaction to what's going on at the moment.

Sitting Down

- *Does he straddle the chair in a backwards fashion?* This deliberate posturing is an attempt to appear special and somehow superior. Yet, for all its insolence, it is a position that protects the sitter and thus reveals a certain vulnerability.

- *Does he sling one leg over a chair arm?* He's telling the world that he's cool and relaxed, taking everything in stride. Question: Is he truly relaxed, or is he masking an inner insecurity?

- *Does he sit with legs crossed, hands behind his head?* This is the classic stance of the bored and/or supremely confident. But there is a double message being sent: on one hand, he's exposing his chest area, which is what alpha dogs and other pack leaders of the animal kingdom dare to do; on the other hand, he's protecting himself below the waist. You be the judge.

- *Does he lean slightly forward, with arms and legs relaxed?* He's hedging his bets. He will accept you and treat you as an equal as long as you return the favor.

Standing

- *Does he put his hands on his hips?* A dominant posture, this can either indicate extreme confidence, minor defensiveness, or underlying anger.

- *Does he fold his arms in front of his chest?* This self-protective stance radiates mistrust. He won't open up until he's absolutely convinced that you deserve his energy and attention.

- *Does he put his arms behind his back?* Even though it doesn't appear to have an ounce of aggressiveness, this is a take-charge posture that is usually adopted by those who are in complete control of the situation at hand.

- *Does he keep his arms relaxed at his sides?* Calm and confident, this position indicates a secure person who is ready for open, honest dialogue.

Sitting at His Desk

- *Does he lean his head on one hand?* This usually means that he's distracted and not really paying attention to what's going on.

- *Does he plant both his elbows in front of him, with his hands and fingers meeting in a steeple position?* He's alert and fairly interested in what you're saying, yet a wee bit cautious.

- *Does he lean slightly forward, with his hands resting on the desk surface?* He's fully tuned in, wanting to hear what you have to say and ready to respond.

Shaking Hands

- *Does he extend his fingers only?* This is a hesitant handshake. In business situations, it may signify that he is unsure of you or perhaps even intimidated; yet it can also send the message that he'd rather be hugging you or nuzzling your neck than giving you a hearty handshake.

- *Does he shake with your hand on top?* Surprisingly, this is a dominant handshake that puts him in charge — in his mind, anyway.

- *Does he grasp your hands with both of his?* This enthusiastic handshake is designed to flatter. It sends a message that you're special.

- *Does he create an equal grip with your hand and his?* The most honest of handshakes, this one projects equality and mutual trust.

Body Language at a Glance

- If he's rubbing his hands together . . . he's excited and very much in the moment.

- If he's tapping his fingers on a table or other surface . . . he's bored or distracted.

- If he's touching his face . . . he feels self-conscious or not in control of the situation.

- If he's partially or fully covering his eyes . . . he's impatient and wants to move on to the next subject or circumstance.

SEX FORECASTING

We try to be ladylike, but in the throes of a major crush, even uptight schoolmarms can't help but wonder: Is he any good in bed? There are ways to find out besides calling up his ex-girlfriends and pumping them for details.

Body language experts believe that people give off physical clues that mirror their sexual styles. When you check out your man, try seeing him through new eyes, using the following theories as your guide.

Posture

- A sloppy, slumped-over posture can indicate a lack of physical confidence; this guy is probably a bit timid and may not take the lead in bed.

- If a man has a relaxed posture and uses plenty of range of motion when he's in the vertical mode, chances are he'll do the same in the horizontal mode.

- A highly controlled posture is one indication of a controlling nature. It's likely that he's a guy who wants to call the shots.

Speech

Speech patterns are an indication of rhythm. If both of you are fast talkers, great. But if you're slow and considered in your speech, and he's a verbal racehorse, it's not a great sign. If the two of you can get into a comfortable conversational rhythm, the prospect of mutual physical rhythm is good.

Touch

- A man who touches you easily and often during conversation is probably a sensual, affectionate guy who is in touch with, well, touch. Just what you want.

- If he's stiff and standoffish or flinches when he's touched, he's either scared to death or physically inhibited. Warming him up will be quite a challenge and may not be worth the effort in the long run.

- The guy who touches himself all the time—you know, he runs his fingers through his hair, rubs his chin, adjusts his clothing, crosses and uncrosses his legs—is either charmingly self-conscious or just plain vain. Self-conscious men need a bit of coaxing. Vain men are often selfish and emotionally distant under the covers.

Social Gestures

- The guy who runs to open doors and pull out chairs is a rare gem. But if he orders your meal off a menu without your input, makes detailed arrangements without consulting you, or tells you what to wear or how to act, he's the controlling type. He just might elect himself Ruler of the Relationship and assign you the role of Arm Candy. Unless you're a passive hero-worshipper, this union doesn't point toward sexual symmetry.

- Is *gallant* an alien word to him? Is he oblivious to your needs? Does it not even occur to him to offer you his jacket when you're shivering in the cold? If so, he could be self-centered and uninterested in you as a person, sexual or otherwise. Or, he could be a decent yet inexperienced guy in need of a woman to teach him the finer points of courtship and romance.

- Some men always call if they're going to be late . . . drop you off at the restaurant before searching for a parking space . . . and gently tell you if you have broccoli in your teeth. This combination of honesty and kindness is known as consideration, and the man who possesses it is likely a great companion, whether you're making conversation, making love, or making breakfast.

THE SECRET LANGUAGE OF SLEEP POSITIONS

Maybe it's a little early for you to investigate the sleeping patterns of your Prince Charming–elect. Maybe not. In any case, there is a large and colorful collection of theories that seek to decode the significance of sleep positions. These ideas are more or less divided into two categories: The hidden meaning behind how a man sleeps when he is alone in bed and the hidden meaning behind how a couple sleeps together. (Please note that we do mean sleep, as in forty winks, sawing logs, lost in dreamland, down for the count.)

The Slumbering Man and His Four Major Sleep Positions

1. **HE SLEEPS ON HIS SIDE IN A FULL FETAL PO-SITION.** He's probably sensitive, emotional, and ex-

pressive. As a true romantic, he considers relationships to be profoundly important to him—which may, in extreme circumstances, cause him to be overly possessive. He has an artistic nature, and in his working life he values personal satisfaction over financial or material rewards.

Curled up and sleeping on one arm means he's gentle, polite, loving, and that he could use a boost of self-confidence.

2. HE SLEEPS ON HIS SIDE WITH HIS KNEES BENT. It's likely that he's flexible, even tempered, compassionate, and sincere. His basic stability and inner peacefulness make him well suited to long-term relationships; in fact, he will probably mate for life. He's also good with money and great at resolving conflicts.

On his right side with his right arm stretched upward could very well indicate that he's blessed with power and good fortune.

On his side with one knee bent usually means that he's prone to nervousness and possibly even whining.

3. HE SLEEPS ON HIS BACK WITH HIS HANDS AT HIS SIDE. Experts deem him outgoing, charming, sociable, and self-confident. He loves power and the perks that come with it, and tends to be generous and fun-loving. As long as he keeps his ego in check, he's a king who can make a great life for his queen.

On his back with his arms and legs spread-eagled means that he loves comfort, beauty, freedom, personal indulgences, and gossip. Luckily, he earns every luxury he gets.

On his back with his legs crossed could mean that he's self-centered and resistant to change. This sleeper needs plenty of "alone" time.

4. HE SLEEPS ON HIS STOMACH WITH HIS ARMS EXTENDED. Chances are he's a perfectionist with a scientific mind who likes to keep everything organized and running smoothly. His ideal relationship has a built-in division of labor—he does his job, you do yours, and all is well. Depend on him for excellent long-term planning, in every sense of the word.

On his stomach with his arms at his side suggests a guarded and secretive nature, but it can also be interpreted as shyness.

A Couple at Rest and Their Five Major Sleep Positions

1. THE SPOON. You both sleep on your side; he curls around you or you curl around him. Experts say that this is the most common sleep position in the first three to five years of a relationship. It creates a safe, protective, and loving sleep environment, and reflects a state of intimacy that is at once physical, emotional, and spiritual.

2. THE HUG. You sleep face to face, wrapped up in each other's limbs. The Hug is romantic but more of a celebratory position that usually doesn't—and probably shouldn't—last through the night. That's okay. It's an expression of shared joy that's as rare and intoxicating as a glass of fine champagne. Get it whenever you can.

3. THE CRADLE. He lies on his back; you snuggle on your side in the crook of his shoulder. This speaks of a strong commitment and a sense of trusting communion. You can also try the Reverse Cradle, where he's still on his back and you are face down at his side, your arm draped across his torso. Either way, it's a sign of a solid and loving union.

4. THE COMFORTING TOUCH. There's nothing wrong with needing your space. This position finds you and your loved one each on your own side of the bed, yet making contact via a foot, a leg, an arm, a hand, or both of your rear ends. Sleeping this way means that you're both secure and independent yet able to maintain an ongoing emotional current.

5. THE ABYSS. Do you and your bedmate avoid touching each other while you sleep? Though such behavior could be a natural reaction to an over-heated apartment, excessive snoring, or an occasional unresolved argument, it could also mean that there's trouble in paradise. Our sleeping selves sometimes act out feelings that we repress in our waking hours. Clinging to opposite edges of the bed, night after night, may indicate that changes need to be made.

INTERIOR MOTIVES

It is said that a man's home is his castle (even if it's a hovel). For the astute woman, a man's home can also be a treasure map that leads to his soul.

Have you gotten a good look at his place? Have you noticed his furniture, floor coverings, window treatments, lighting, wall art, colors, and knickknacks (a.k.a. decorative accessories)? If so, you're ready to get a good look at the inside of his head.

Here, we offer four archetypal decorating styles. Find the one that most closely matches the style of the guy you're eyeballing, and read all about him.

A few pointers, before you start:

1. Analyze permanent living spaces only. Ignore summer rentals, dorm rooms, sublets, etc.

2. If he lives with a roommate or two or three, focus your study on a private space, such as his bedroom.

3. Don't judge a place that was decorated by his ex, his mother, or a design professional.

The Modern Male

His home may have:

- A minimalist, modernist aesthetic

- Equipment on display (computer, TV, DVD player, stereo, treadmill, etc.)

- Very little clutter

- A lack of color

- CDs arranged in alphabetical order

- Blinds rather than curtains on the windows

- Wall-to-wall carpeting or industrial flooring (no scatter rugs)

- Furniture made of glass, metal, or leather

- General cleanliness and organization

- Black-and-white photos as art

- Few or no personal mementos in sight

Analysis

The true Modern Male isn't known for being warm and fuzzy — but that doesn't mean he isn't a good catch. This man is careful about his choices and follows a path of well-defined goals. He's interested in having the best, which applies to his possessions as well as his personal life. Though during his single-hood he may indulge in casual flings here and there, he's serious about finding "the one." When he meets the right woman, he'll woo her with intense determination and will dedicate himself to creating a rock-solid partnership built on trust, mutual respect, and, of course, everlasting love.

The Modern Male may take you on a date to . . .
a new, ultrahip restaurant for dinner, followed by a show at a jazz club, to which he has excellent tickets.

The Modern Male gift of love:
an exclusive designer watch or purse, or a stylish little cell phone.

Nature Boy

His home may have:

- A cozy, comfy aesthetic

- A mix of furniture comprised of hand-me-downs, restored castoffs, and handcrafted pieces

- Sheer curtains, no curtains, or matchstick blinds on windows

- A color palette of earthy tones, such as sage green, brown, rust, and beige

- Wood floors with area rugs

- Living plants

- Natural materials, such as wood, rattan, wicker, and sisal

- Engaging items on display, including family photos, pottery, antiques, textiles, and sentimental relics

Analysis

Nature Boy is a kind, affectionate, relaxed sort of guy who aspires to live simply and honestly. He's nonmaterialistic and finds his happiness in intangibles such as family, social activism, the great outdoors, and eternal love. As a partner, he is passionate, communicative, and committed, and has a talent for sharing on all levels. Though he may never be a millionaire, he is a good-hearted man who can establish and grow a stable, peaceful home life with a down-to-earth woman.

Nature Boy might take you on a date to . . .
  his place, where he'll cook a meal for you, then
  lead you to the rooftop for some stargazing.

The Nature Boy gift of love:
  something he made with his own hands — a
  mahogany bench, a silver brooch, a pair of snow-
  shoes, a loaf of Irish soda bread.

Mr. Civilized

His home may have:

  - An old-world, somewhat formal aesthetic

  - A collection of furniture comprised of heir-
  looms, fine antiques, and European-style pieces

  - Electronic equipment hidden in armoires and
  behind closed cabinets

  - Oriental rugs on polished floors

  - A crown jewels palette (ruby, sapphire,
  emerald, platinum, gold)

  - Soft lighting generated by lamps

  - Framed paintings on walls

  - Books (no paperbacks) on display in cases and
  built-in shelves

  - Symmetrical arrangements of objets d'art on
  side tables, fireplace mantels, etc.

Analysis

Mr. Civilized is sophisticated and cultured, but underneath that refined exterior lurks a hopeless romantic who yearns to play the role of Prince Charming. Unfortunately for him, he's sensitive almost to the point of being fragile. In fact, his home is his sanctuary, where he holes up to protect himself from the noisy, crass world outside. The woman who is invited into his private sanctum would be wise to take her time and mind her manners. If all goes well, she just might become his queen and be gifted with a lifetime of romance and devotion.

Mr. Civilized might take you on a date to . . .
a gala, black-tie fund-raiser held at a spectacular venue.

The Mr. Civilized gifts of love:
a dozen long-stemmed red roses at first; later, sparkling baubles in black velvet boxes.

Man Alive

His home may have:

- A lively aesthetic that's constantly evolving

- Rooms that become workshops, homey nests, studios, or party palaces, as the need arises

- Inventive furnishings created from found

objects (a coffee table with bowling ball legs, easy chairs made from inner tubes, a hospital gurney made into a credenza)

- Nontraditional decorative accessories (mirror ball, cigarette machine, X-ray images, vintage doghouses)

- Interactive items, such as conga drums, a pinball machine, a dartboard, or snow globes

- A deficiency of basic, practical items (towels, lightbulbs, tissues, forks, sofas, bureaus)

- A dramatic, colorful, or heavily patterned palette

- Cluttered surfaces and general disorganization

Analysis

His place is a work in progress, and so is he. The Man Alive guy seeks constant inspiration and excitement, and keeps himself in perpetual motion so as not to miss anything. He has no interest in settling down, at least not on an intellectual or artistic level, but he does need love. The woman who takes on this whirling dervish must be independent and grounded, willing to hold down the fort while he bounces back and forth between victory, defeat, exhilaration, and despair. If she's lucky, he'll find a niche where his mad genius can thrive. In any case, she'll never be bored.

Man Alive might take you on a date to . . .
>a gallery opening, then a tiny ethnic restaurant in an obscure neighborhood, then a club where a friend of his is playing.

The Man Alive gift of love:
>something surprising and offbeat, such as a bag of marbles, a live turtle, or a trip to Fiji.

WHAT YOU'RE LOOKING FOR MIGHT BE IN HIS REFRIGERATOR

While you're snooping around his place, take a peek inside his fridge. Though the contents of cool-erators (as Chuck Berry called them) change on a daily basis, you can probably get a basic idea of what kinds of foods your man keeps on hand. And that information, my darlings, is yet another way to hook up a monitor to his secret heart.

- If he has a near-empty fridge that contains to-go cartons, a few beers, a lonely bottle of ketchup, rolls of film, and other temporary and/or nonperishable items, then you're probably dealing with a guy who uses his place as a pit stop. Though it's doubtful your man will cook you a gourmet meal anytime soon, this fridge is the sign of an ambitious man who is thinking of the future, and who is no doubt working toward a real life and a real home that he can build with the woman of his dreams.

- If he has a refrigerator populated by wholesome, natural foods and nutritional supplements, he is a man who cares about his health and body. Longevity is an excellent goal for both of you; be aware, however, that your relationship with this guy might hinge on your compatible habits. When a vegan meets a carnivore, something's got to give.

- Is his fridge stocked with champagne, caviar, and other fancy stuff? Then he's either (a) trying to impress you or (b) the kind of guy who keeps seductive provisions on hand in order to impress any woman that happens to show up. If you can't pinpoint his intentions, then follow your heart. You might choose to believe that he's a guy who will shower you with the best that life has to offer; or you might think that champagne and caviar are tired romantic clichés. In which case you can inspire him to be more original. Or you can walk away.

- What if his refrigerator door opens upon a cornucopia of produce, meats, cheeses, and exotic condiments? Well then, you've probably got yourself a guy who loves to cook. Such a man is a rare and wonderful find; not only is he self-sufficient and a natural caregiver, he also has a heightened sensuality that can mean good things for you, in more ways than one.

PALM PILOT: HOW TO IDENTIFY
THE ELEMENTAL HANDS

You might think you know yourself—or your man—like the back of your hand. But it's the palm of the hand that tells the real story.

It isn't necessary to conduct an up-close reading of lines or mounts to get a bead on a person's character. In elemental palm identification, the general shape of the whole hand—palm, fingers, thumb—can be interpreted at a glance.

The Earth Hand

Look for a broad hand with a wide palm, short fingers, and simple lines.

The Earth Hand is associated with people who are practical, hard working, honest, stable, and enjoy making things and being productive, especially in a physical way. They're likely to be orderly and tenacious, but may lack imagination. This hand is linked with the astrological signs of Taurus, Virgo, and Capricorn.

The Water Hand

Look for long fingers, a narrow palm with subtle lines, and a delicate or graceful overall shape.

This palm indicates a person who is highly sensitive to other people and his environment, and who might be receptive to the point of being psychic. Mood changes are many and are triggered by immediate stimuli. The Water Hand is associated with the signs of Cancer, Scorpio, and Pisces.

The Fire Hand

Look for a narrow palm with short fingers and well-defined lines.

This is the palm of a passionate extrovert who is warm, intuitive, active, and creative. On the downside, he may be hot-tempered or emotionally unpredictable. The astrological signs of Aries, Leo, and Sagittarius are related to the Fire Hand.

The Air Hand

Look for a strongly structured hand with a wide palm, long fingers, and prominent lines.

The Air Hand belongs to a powerful communicator who is intellectual and nonemotional, and given to reason and logic, but who is also confident and full of hope. Gemini, Libra, and Aquarius are the astrological air signs associated with this type of hand.

HANDWRITING ANALYSIS

Professional graphologists are sometimes hired by the FBI to help solve heinous crimes. When they're called into the service of their country, they study handwriting samples with the dedication of research scientists and analyze every tick and twitch of penmanship before presenting a profile of the writer's personality and character.

When amateurs like us attempt to analyze the handwriting of a friend, loved one, or potential loved one, we're most successful when we focus on a few dominant letterforms and learn which traits they're associated with.

Think of the following as your starter kit to handwriting analysis.

Catch and Release

When lowercase letters *a*, *c*, or *d* have a hook that could snag a wide-mouth bass, you can be pretty sure that the writer is attracted to those who play "hard to get." The hook is formed by a straight upward stroke, whose path is crossed by a curved downward stroke. Optimists say that the writer doesn't back away from a challenge; pessimists predict that this man will quickly become bored after he gets the girl.

In the Driver's Seat

The man who crosses his lowercase *t*s with a downward slant (sloping toward the right) is likely to be dominant or domineering. At best, this could mean he's a take-charge kind of guy; at worst, it could mean he's a control freak, or even a bully.

An Army of One

Do you know what a descender is? In calligraphy, it describes the lower half of letters such as *g, j, q, y,* and sometimes *f.* When written in longhand, each of these descenders should have a loop. If that loop is so tightly rendered that it traces over itself and ends up looking like a single line, it could mean that the writer is a loner who doesn't trust others. It could also be a sign of independence, or it might indicate that he fears intimate relationships.

Thin Skin

When ascenders — that is, the upper half of letters *b, d, f, h, k,* and/or *t* — have big fat loops, the person in question might be overly sensitive to criticism. Sensitivity is a lovely trait, unless it morphs into defensiveness, suspicion or, at worst, paranoia.

NEW MATH NUMEROLOGY

This ancient system of divination assigns numbers to letters and finds meaning in reductive mathematics. Never mind the complicated back story: Here, we present an easy way to get a quick reading on your beloved's "soul urge" — that is, the basic motive that drives his actions and the direction of his life.

Do you have a pen and sheet of paper ready? Good.

STEP 1: Spell out his first, middle (if you know it), and last name in clear capital letters.

STEP 2: Using the following chart as your guide, write down the corresponding number under each vowel in his name. (Note: Only include *Y* if it's pronounced as a vowel, as in Billy and Dylan. Don't use it when it's pronounced as a consonant, as in Yuri and Young.)

 A = 1
 Ɛ = 5
 I = 9
 O = 6
 U = 3
 y = 7

STEP 3: Total the numbers. If the resulting sum is ten or more, add the two digits together. If the total is still more than ten, add up the new digits (see examples below for full clarification). The final single-digit number represents his soul urge.

Example A:
1. Say his name is Bob Smith.

2. The O has a value of 6; the I has a value of 9.

3. Six plus 9 equal 15.

4. In numerology, double-digit numbers must be reduced to single-digit numbers; this is done by adding up the two digits. Thus, 15 becomes 1 plus 5, which total 6.

5. Bob Smith's soul urge number is 6.

Example B:
1. You want to know more about a guy named Sammy Jones.

2. The A has a value of 1; the Y, because it is a vowel sound, counts as 7; the O has a value of 6; and the E has a value of 5. Add them all together, you get 19.

3. To reduce the double-digit number, add the 1 and the 9. This equals 10. Still too many digits! Thus, you must add the 1 and the 0.

4. Your grand total is 1, which is Sammy Jones's soul urge number.

STEP 4: Now that you've figured out the significant number in that special someone's life, it's payoff time. Sit back and bask in the wisdom of numerology.

Numerology Soul Urges

1. Individuality

This person aspires to be creative, independent, original, and courageous, and to fill leadership positions. He's got all the right skills in his personal toolbox; if he's internally off-kilter, however, he might come off as egotistical, stubborn, or overbearing.

2. Harmony and Diplomacy

Charm, adaptability, and receptiveness are his gifts; he also shows an affinity for music and rhythm. When not at his best, he could become oversensitive, cowardly, or even deceptive.

3. Expression

Artistic self-expression is what this person strives for, and he gets ahead by using his natural optimism, sociability, and charm. At his worst, the Number 3 character is vain, superficial, extravagant, and jealous.

4. Practicality and Discipline

This type prides himself on being hardworking and disciplined. His talents include dependability, dignity, carefulness, and endurance. To succeed, he must steer away from negative feelings that may render him narrow-minded, rigid, or heartless.

5. Freedom

Sometimes called the "number of man," this reading indicates a person who wants freedom and variety in life. He is most likely curious, clever, and versatile, but his natural joie de vivre puts him in danger of becoming irresponsible, self-indulgent, and/or insensitive.

6. Home and Service

The Number 6 man is ruled by a desire to heal or protect others. He seeks love and harmony, and is a conscientious, idealistic, and sympathetic soul. When threatened or deeply unhappy, he has the potential to become anxious, meddling, suspicious, or cynical.

7. *Analysis and Wisdom*

This introspective person yearns for inner peace and wisdom, and tends to find satisfaction in scientific and technical arenas. Though usually refined and poised, he is susceptible to sarcastic, aloof, melancholy, nervous, or deceitful behavior.

8. *Material Success and Power*

He's a born executive and can use his qualities of self-reliance, natural ability, control, and good judgment to achieve great success. The downside is that he risks becoming materialistic, overly ambitious, hard-hearted, and unscrupulous.

9. *Understanding and Completeness*

The Number 9 character may very well possess such qualities as compassion, artistic talent, selflessness, a sense of brotherhood, a universal world view . . . all of which add up to a soul urge for completeness — or, perhaps, an understanding of human nature. When these lofty ideals go wrong, he might instead exhibit egocentricity, impracticality, displaced emotionalism, or vulgarity.

THE I CHING, SORT OF

For more than 3,000 years, the I Ching (pronounced "ee ching")—which is both a book and a mystical practice — has been a profound presence in China. Not only is it a cornerstone of the country's general philosophies (including Confucianism and Taoism), it has also served as an oracle to countless numbers of seekers, from kings to peasants, who have consulted its guidance on matters great and small.

The most respected English-language version of the I Ching, or Book of Changes, was introduced in the 1920s by Richard Wilhelm. Still very much in print, and now bearing various prefaces — one written by Carl Jung himself — the book is some 750 pages long (with tiny type, mind you) and is a must-read for any serious student of the discipline.

Proper practitioners of the I Ching connect with its eternal wisdom by casting coins or sticks, which are interpreted into a figure of six lines. Some lines are solid, some are broken, and some are "changing," depending on how the coins or sticks are thrown. What results is one of sixty-four figures, each of which carries its own complex meaning.

For those of us with short attention spans, there are unorthodox shortcuts that tap into the secrets of the I Ching but don't require serious study. We could use them to know ourselves better; for the purposes of this book, however, we're going to exploit the lessons of the I Ching in order to improve our love lives.

What's His Sign, and What Does He Want?

You can conduct this exercise face to face, in a private setting, or you can be a witchy woman and do it all by yourself, without his knowledge. All you need to know is the date and year of his birth.

STEP ONE: Determine whether his day of birth is an odd or an even number. For instance, if he was born on May 17, 1966, his day of birth is 17, an odd number. If he was born on October 26, 1970, his day of birth is 26, an even number.

An odd number indicates a yang day. This is symbolized by a solid, horizontal line.

————————————————————

YANG

An even number means he was born on a yin day. This is symbolized by a horizontal line with a break in the middle.

STEP TWO: Look at the year of his birth. Does it end in an odd number? If so, that means he was born in a yang year (solid line). Make a note.

If his year of birth ends in an even number, that indicates a yin year (broken line).

STEP THREE: Match his results with the first two columns of the following chart, then look to the third column for his divining symbol.

DAY OF BIRTH	+	YEAR OF BIRTH	=	I CHING SIGN
yang (odd)	+	yang (odd)	=	——————— YANG
yang (odd)	+	yin (even)	=	———✕——— YANG changing into YIN
yin (even)	+	yin (even)	=	——— ——— YIN
yin (even)	+	yang (odd)	=	——◯—— YIN changing into YANG

His I Ching Sign

YANG

Yang

This man is solid, strong, hardworking, and hard-playing. He gravitates to power and tends to attract money, but at heart he is a family man who takes the role of provider very seriously. Though he probably has plenty of male friends, he relates well to women. His ideal mate is a wife, a mother (for himself as well as children), and a good cook.

YANG changing into YIN

Yang Changing into Yin

He's a conqueror. Smooth on the outside and tough on the inside, he goes after what he wants and doesn't shy away from conflicts. This is a man who works out, plays rough, spends money freely, and seizes opportunities to be a hero. When it comes to relationships, he seeks a woman who is both a wife and a mistress. To him, sex is a reward, and he's cursed with a roving eye — though whether he acts on his urges or not is up to him.

Yin

Cool. Refined. Fiercely territorial. The yin man is both a gentleman and a calculating politician who uses his natural charisma to pull off the best deals he can (especially those that involve real estate or luxury goods). He can charm people from all walks of life and easily gain their trust. When it comes to romance, he'll settle down with a (preferably curvaceous and busty) woman who can be a perfect public partner as well as a caring lover.

YIN changing into YANG

Yin Changing into Yang

This yin/yang man has a strong inner life and judges his success by how much he's learned. Still waters run deep: Though he might appear strong and silent, he's sensitive and gentle on the inside. He is apt to come to the rescue of others in need, and tends to work more than he plays. To him, sex is spiritual, and he seeks a woman who believes in him and who knows how to "read" his innermost thoughts and desires.

LEFT BRAIN/RIGHT BRAIN

Your brain, and the brain of everyone you know, has two distinct halves — one on the left, and one on the right — called hemispheres. Though connected by fibers that allow them to pool their talents, each hemisphere is hardwired to handle certain jobs. The left hemisphere is associated with verbal skills, logic, sequence, mathematics, and all things analytical and intellectual. The right hemisphere is assigned to more intuitive and sensuous tasks; it is responsible for processing emotions and interpreting nonverbal cues, and it is the birthplace of feelings.

This right/left distinction isn't a load of hooey. In fact, the two hemispheres of the brain are physiologically distinct. The left side is mostly made up of tightly packed gray matter, where neurons are in close contact and positioned to tackle intricate, detailed problems. The right side has more white matter and a loose arrangement that allows for creative connections with distant-cousin neurons.

Most people are either right-brained or left-brained. Their primary hemisphere directs much of their behavior and influences their choices in strange and wonderful ways.

Can left-brained people get along with right-brained people? Sure, but it's a great help to learn which type is which and to recognize the essential differences of each. Such knowledge can open the doors to communication and prevent basic misunderstandings.

You Might Be a Left-Brainer if You . . .

- work as a scientist, accountant, financial adviser, programmer, fact checker, researcher, technician, etc.

- regularly read newspapers, magazines, or nonfiction books, but rarely read novels

- are fascinated by engines, computers, machinery, or systems in general

- would rather be an architect than an interior designer

- have a way with words and prefer clever turns of phrases over sentimental outpourings

- hate being late

- would rather be a surgeon than a nurse

- put your faith in facts rather than feelings or hunches

- enjoy making detailed plans and locking them in

- would rather design a recording studio than be a talent scout

You Might Be a Right-Brainer if You . . .

- prefer art and poetry to math and science

- have an artistic, creative, or humanistic job (e.g., counselor, teacher, caretaker, craftsperson, chef, recruiter)

- believe in the power of imagination and intuition

- would never sign up to be a quiz show contestant

- aren't particularly organized

- have vivid dreams while sleeping *and* awake

- are more likely to rent a movie than watch CNN

- aren't known for being punctual

- would rather be a costume designer than an executive director

- naturally think in pictures and images, and have a hard time focusing on numbers

How the Two Shall Meet

If you're a left-brained person who wants to make an impression on a right-brained person, try . . .

- treating him to sensual, physical pleasures, such as a gourmet dinner, a bike ride along woodsy paths, a salsa dance lesson, or a trip to an amusement park

- sharing personal, emotional intimacies; though it may be difficult for you to wear your heart on your sleeve, the rightie will put you at ease and see the whole picture

- listening with empathy and patience, even if he seems to be speaking in haiku; right-brained people are grateful for your ability to interpret, analyze, and crystallize their sometimes scattered thoughts

If you're a right-brainer who wants to connect with a left-brained person, try . . .

- asking for help with a vexing problem that requires logic and know-how to solve

- inviting him to an intellectually stimulating event, such as a lecture by a renowned philosopher, a guided tour of historical sites, or a documentary film festival

- allowing the left-brainer to teach you about one of his favorite subjects, be it baseball, astronomy, politics, whatever

KEEP YOUR EYES ON THE ROAD RAGE

It's possible that a man's driving style says everything about him. Slow and cautious might mean that he's a timid fellow who's wary of moving too fast in a relationship. Fast and focused could indicate an ambitious guy who knows what he wants—

in life and in love — and is determined to make it happen.

One thing's for sure: The man who pitches fits while driving has an explosive temper. Though he might be perfectly charming and gentlemanly toward you, his girlie-girl, it's very possible that his road rage could turn into office rage, yard rage, kitchen rage, or bedroom rage. And that's a bad trip for you.

Assuming you've been his passenger at least five times, the following yes-or-no questions should help you decide whether to lean back and enjoy the ride or make him pull over and let you out.

Have you ever seen your guy:

1. Go through a red light because there were no other cars at the intersection?
2. Give the finger to another driver?
3. Get into an altercation over a parking space?
4. Be rude or confrontational to a police officer who pulled him over?
5. Chase a car that cut him off in traffic?
6. Lean on his horn when someone in front of him dawdled at a green light?
7. Flash his lights at or tailgate a slow driver in order to force the person to let him pass?
8. Tear up a parking ticket?

Answer Key

We hope you didn't answer yes to four or more questions. Three or fewer yes answers are okay, because it's natural to get hot under the collar once in awhile, especially if you spend way too many hours of your life in a car. But four or more yes responses indicate increasingly dangerous levels of road rage.

My advice: Avoid getting involved with the guy who turns into a street-fighting man the minute he gets behind the wheel. Chronic road-ragers use aggression and violence to relieve their stress; as any junior psychologist will tell you, that is not a healthy coping strategy. What's more, many road-rage guys believe that they're superior to the riffraff that surrounds them on highways and byways. (Some even think they're above the law, or ought to be.) They resort to intimidation — the preferred technique of school-yard bullies — to clear a path so they can be at the head of the pack. Beware. This man could be dangerous for you on many levels.

If you're hopelessly in love with a road-rager, try to diffuse his anger by: (1) convincing him to get a job within walking distance from home; (2) signing him up for kickboxing classes; (3) buying him an electric car that has no pickup whatsoever; or (4) supplying him with action-, adventure-, or erotic-themed books on tape to listen to while he drives.

THE TRUTH ABOUT DOGS, CATS, AND FISH

Does your guy have a fuzzy mutt, a tank of tropical fish, a favorite pussycat, or a house full of strays? The pets we keep are a reflection of our inner selves. While you're getting closer to your man, take the time to observe his interactions with animals. Ye shall know him by his critters, as Shakespeare never said.

Dogs

The dog-owning man is generally affectionate and demonstrative — just like Rover or Spot. But canines come in many shapes and sizes, and serve many roles. See which of the following categories best describes the relationship between your guy and his furry pal.

THE WEEKEND WARRIOR. Does your fella have a large or medium-size dog that he runs, hikes, climbs, bikes, swims, or camps with? If so, the animal is probably a surrogate for male friendship, and chances are the man in your life has chosen the dog because it's easy to get along with, always listens, is ready for action at the jingle of a leash, doesn't drink, isn't boring, and won't embarrass him or hit on you. This man/dog relationship suggests an independent guy who is capable of sharing, craves action, and has plenty of love to give. Your job is to bond with the dog right away so that you can become part of an adventurous threesome. Warning: The Weekend Warrior and his dog can be irresistible to lots of women besides you; thus, it's wise to lavish the dog with affection, treats, toys, and rides in the car in order to gain the hound's total devotion.

DOGGY DADDY. Small breeds are the Doggy Daddy's favorites. He loves coming home to one or more frantic little dogs that go crazy when they see him. In turn, he fusses over them, carries them in his arms, talks to them in silly voices, and enjoys spoiling them. The Doggy Daddy might be gay. Or, he might be a straight man who likes it when pretty, fluffy creatures are dependent on him. Being the "parent" is his turn-on; in romantic relations, this tendency might manifest itself in controlling or smothering behavior. Hopefully, though, it just means this guy likes to pamper women and make them feel special.

THE INVESTOR. Some men keep dogs as status symbols or for financial gains. The Investor may have one or two expensive, pedigree dogs that he puts through obedience school, meticulous veterinary checkups, and routine groomings. He probably also crates them at night, feeds them nutritional supplements, and breeds them in order to sell the puppies. If he's willing to reject a pet because it compulsively chews shoes or has a bad hip, then he's a shallow guy who values profit and rank over emotional connections. If he falls in love with his dogs, however, it shows his true heart. This kindly Investor might be demanding and hardheaded on the outside but has a core of warmth and compassion. He's probably worth pursuing, as long as you can initially impress him with your fine breeding and excellent form.

THE RESCUER. He's a guy who will rescue a skinny mutt from the street or adopt a mongrel from a shelter on the day it's scheduled to be put down. If the dog has been abandoned, neglected, or abused, the Rescuer will nurse it back to health and be rewarded with lifelong loyalty. Often, the Rescuer is a shy or socially awkward man who relates to an unloved dog as a fellow outsider. He thrives on the unconditional love of his four-legged companion and often forms an emotional bond with the animal that, to him, is more stable than most of his human relationships. As a romantic partner, the Rescuer is sensitive almost to a fault, and doesn't easily trust others. If you are a patient and understanding woman, you might rescue the Rescuer and gain access to his deep, intimate, and fiercely committed soul.

Cats

Beautiful, graceful, and independent. Sometimes haughty, sometimes hilarious, often comforting, always unpredictable. Cats are more like housemates than pets. As it is with dogs, however, there are all kinds of felines and all kinds of men who love them. Study the dynamics between your man and his cat(s), and you'll soon develop a clear snapshot of his psyche.

ONE-CAT MAN. Whether he bought it as a kitten or inherited it from a former roommate, this man has a strong attachment to a particular cat. He probably isn't a "cat guy," and might not respond to other felines at all, but he does share his domain with a quiet partner who perches on windowsills, sits on the newspaper, and asks to be petted now and then. The One-Cat Man appreciates his pet's personality and beauty, and he likes having it around the house, but he doesn't demand its attention. He brings a similar dynamic to love relationships: He respects his woman's independence and is perfectly happy to give space and get space, then join her at the end of the day for some stroking and purring.

MR. SOFTIE. He can't stand turning his back on animals in need. He might rehabilitate orphaned birds and wounded raccoons, but his real weakness is for stray cats. His pattern usually begins with a simple act of kindness, such as retrieving a starving kitten from a Dumpster. Cats don't require much maintenance, so when a second stray is rescued from the side of the highway, he gives it a home. Mr. Softie loves seeing his cats evolve from desperation to contentment; sooner or later, a third needy feline will be introduced to his household. If the cat collection stops there, then you can deem Mr. Softie a caring man who is dedicated to family life and who might be a great candidate for fathering or adopting children. If his gaggle of strays keeps growing, however, beware. He could have an addictive personality and might end up with twenty-eight cats and a summons from the health department.

FANCY-CAT FANCIER. This man is enchanted by the mystery and history of cats. He's drawn to elite breeds—no matter how persnickety and demanding they might be—and is more than happy to lavish them with attention and expensive care. Never mind if the cat in question doesn't return his love. He thinks of his pedigree cat as a precious asset, even if the finicky feline refuses to purr or procreate. Do you detect a slightly masochistic pattern here? In the romantic arena, the Fancy-Cat Fancier tends to worship women from afar and is prone to taking on "trophy" girlfriends, who look good on his arm and accept his gifts, yet have nothing to say to him. There is a cure for this syndrome: loads of loving contact from a genuine woman who can help him achieve sincere communication.

Fish

This is where science and aesthetics collide. The man who keeps tropical fish must create and maintain a miniature ecosystem in which colorful vertebrates can survive. It's as much about the tank as it is about the finned critters.

THE AQUAMANIAC. Whether he has a freshwater or saltwater tank, the dedicated aquarium keeper has to be a chemical genius as well as an expert in the science of fish habits and behaviors. The result of his labors is a gorgeous display that rivals snorkeling expeditions in coral reefs. As a boyfriend or a husband, this man will keep the homefront organized and operating smoothly. Maintaining a clean tank, healthy fish, correct water temperature, and a perfect pH balance requires similar skills to keeping the furnace running, the hedges trimmed, and the books balanced. High-maintenance women, rejoice: The Aquamaniac is accustomed to providing rarefied environments in which beautiful creatures can thrive.

FLIP-FLOPPER. The man whose only pet is a solitary goldfish in a bowl might crave the presence of living creatures around him, but doesn't want to deal with complicated upkeep or long-term commitments. Goldfish are usually temporary pets that suit temporary lifestyles. The man in question might be waiting to find his true home as defined by a woman he loves.

Interactive Intelligence Gathering

Everybody loves undivided attention. As a woman, you're treated to rituals like facials, manicures, and deep conversations with your best friend, in which *you* become the center of the universe (if only for twenty minutes or so).

Men are rarely lavished with such intense personal attention, which is one reason why the following activities are so compelling, so successful, and so, well, sexy.

This chapter is interactive. It asks you to reach out to him in all sorts of ways, including physically (palm reading), subconsciously (The Cube), emotionally (the ex-girlfriend quiz), and playfully ("Well, I Never!"). Are you prepared to throw out leading questions, give him quizzes, and get inside his head while staring into his eyes? And are you prepared to accept his answers?

Very well. Read on.

PALMISTRY FOR THE IMPATIENT

Do you know that the lines in the palms of your hands are constantly changing? To be sure, they change very slowly, so perhaps a better word would be *evolving*. In any case, palmists believe that there is a link between the lines of the hands and the neurological routes of the mind (which also evolve over time).

Palmistry is complicated stuff, and the serious practitioner will interpret all sorts of elements, from the lines around your wrists to the relative lengths of your fingers.

But let's say you just want to take a guy's hand in yours and dazzle him with a quick reading, while stealthily gathering information for your secret files. You can do this by concentrating on the *heart line* and the *head line*. These two major lines may be short or long, curved or relatively straight, and may even intersect with each other.

How to Speed-Read a Palm

1. Take the palm of his left hand in both of your hands, with his fingers pointed toward you. This is the hand you want to read, because it's cross-wired to the right hemisphere of his brain, and

thus represents his emotional, creative, and intuitive side.

2. Locate his **heart line,** which is the horizontal line closest to the base of his fingers. Compare it with the examples below to find its nearest match. Note: If his heart line is more pronounced than his head line, it's a sign that he is ruled more by his emotions than by his intellect. In this case, emphasize heart line readings over head line readings.

- The heart line begins at the base of the forefinger and extends to the left side of the hand in a relatively straight path: *Indicates devotion, affection, sympathy, and compassion. This man is capable of steadfast love.*

- The heart line originates between the forefinger and the middle finger and extends to the left in a gentle or pronounced curve: *He's tolerant and practical, with plenty of common sense when it comes to love; however, it's also likely that he's quite sensual.*

- The heart line begins at the base of the middle finger and extends to the side of the hand in a gentle or pronounced curve: *He's possessed of a*

powerful sex drive and might put his own desires above the needs of others.

3. Locate his **head line.** This horizontal line runs parallel to the heart line and usually begins somewhere between the thumb and the base of the forefinger. If his head line is more prominent than his heart line, it indicates that he is ruled by his intellect rather than by his emotions. In this case, his head line readings carry more weight than his heart line readings.

- The head line originates about halfway between the crook of the thumb and the base of the forefinger (its path across the palm might be curved or straight): *He's cautious and capable, but also high-spirited. The closer to the thumb the head line is, the more imaginative and dream-driven he is.*

- The head line begins smack in the crook of the thumb: *He tends to be a worrywart who is easily influenced by others and might be irritable and argumentative.*

- The head line begins near the base of the forefinger, possibly connecting at that point with the heart line: *This is a born leader who is likely to be ambitious, powerful, and talented, and perhaps also egotistical.*

- The head line and the heart line are joined together or intersect with each other beyond the point of origin: *He might very well be a cool (or even cold) person who is calculating, unfeeling, and dedicated only to himself.*

ASTROLOGICAL PALMISTRY

Secrets to the soul are not only found in the lines of one's hands; they can also be read in the fleshy pads and bumps, known as "mounts," that help make every palm a unique work of art.

Long ago — way before you were born — astrologers named the seven major mounts of the hand after heavenly bodies. These became associated with certain qualities of personality and character. Thus, the protrusions of the palm can provide an intimate map, with the most prominent mount leading the reading.

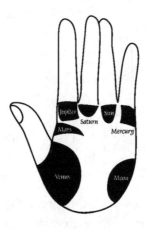

The Mercury Palm has a pronounced Mount of Mercury. When the fingers are spread, the little finger tends to splay outward, distanced from the other digits.

This person is knowledgeable, literate, and quick-witted. He can be quite entertaining in social situations, but tends to value intellectual discourse more than emotional interactions. When it comes to relationships, he wants a woman who can challenge him and grow with him, both mentally and physically.

The Solar (Sun) Palm is generally marked by a well-developed Mount of Sun and a fourth finger that is longer (or as long as) the middle finger.

He's a leader with a strong desire for power and public recognition. Socially charming, engaging, and enthusiastic, he enjoys being the center of attention. In the realm of romance, he may make you feel like a queen and show you the time of your life, but beware: Many a Solar type has been known to treat women as accessories.

The Saturn Palm is marked by a long middle finger arising from a well-padded Mount of Saturn.

The Saturn man tends to be a loner. He is serious and cautious, but might also be self-confident, practical, ambitious, and patient. He has a strong streak of perfectionism that extends to love relationships, which makes him loyal and reliable, but not necessarily exciting or outwardly romantic.

The Jupiter Palm is usually thick and heavily padded, from the fingers to the wrist, and has a distinctly fleshy Mount of Jupiter.

This palm is the mark of an even-tempered person who is tolerant, generous, adventurous, and blessed with incredible luck. In love, the Jupiter man is all fun and games, but not focused on commitment. Unless he's over forty, think of him as a sizzling fling and enjoy the ride.

The Mars Palm features a prominent Mount of Mars, which might be marked by a knob of skin above the thumb joint (most noticeable when the fingers are held together). Mars men often have strong, well-developed thumbs.

Courageous, combative, vital, and alert, the man with this hand often excels at sports and other forms of war. In romantic situations, he rules the roost, appoints himself director and producer of the relationship, and takes on the role of passionate protector.

The Venus Palm can be identified by a meaty Mount of Venus that begins at the base of the thumb and extends nearly to the center of the palm. Don't be surprised if the Venus hand is somewhat small and short-thumbed.

Pleasure and beauty are his guiding principles; it follows that he is artistic, active, personally magnetic, sexually appealing, and easily seduced by attractive environments and situations. With him as a love partner, you can count on him to be fun and imaginative. Just don't expect him to be predictable or reliable.

The Lunar (Moon) Palm is soft and often features many fine lines in addition to a pronounced Mount of the Moon.

This hand belongs to a multifaceted man who is easygoing, dreamy, and likable. He is restless, adventurous, and imaginative, but also extravagant, fearful, and subject to fierce mood swings. He's a cyclical creature, like the Moon itself, and is likely to put his romantic partners through all kinds of changes, wonderful and not.

THUMB READING

Thumb people believe that the key to one's character can be found in the fifth Beatle of the hand—the thumb. Though thumb reading doesn't get the play that palmistry does, it can be a surprisingly revealing exercise. Plus, it's a great excuse to touch someone and can easily be practiced in dark cocktail lounges, the backseats of limousines, and other potentially steamy locations.

- A **long** thumb is as tall as the middle joint of the index finger. The owner of this digit is confident and supportive of others, but has a tendency toward working too hard and exhausting himself.

- A thumb is considered **short** if it doesn't reach the middle knuckle of the index finger. This person is easygoing and can adapt to most any situation. He might have a problem asserting himself or expressing his own needs, so be gentle.

- The **flexible** thumb can easily bend backwards, in classic hitchhiking style. Such a thumb indicates fairness, open-mindedness, and generosity of spirit.

Though he's not afraid to think for himself, he does have the tendency to please others at his own expense.

- A **firm** thumb lacks the backwards range of movement that a flexible thumb has. It likely belongs to a responsible, dependable sort who, at times, can be stubborn and a bit resistant to new ideas.

- Thumbs have three phalanges, which are the fleshy areas between the knuckles. The **first phalange,** which is at the top of the digit where one's thumb print is located, represents will. If this phalange is well developed, this person has a strong mind and spirit, and works hard to get what he wants.

- The **second phalange,** located between the two thumb joints, is all about logic. A meaty second phalange indicates a practical person with a scientific mind who reasons his way through problems. If this same phalange is tapered in the middle (looking as if it has a waist), it means this person has a sense of playfulness and loves people.

- The **last phalange** is part of the palm but is also an extension of the thumb. Known as the Mount of Venus, this phalange is associated with love, passion, and sensuality. The man with a fleshy Mount of Venus is affectionate, sexual . . . a real Romeo.

THE CUBE

This is the perfect interactive quiz to play on a front porch on a lazy afternoon, around a fire on a ski trip, in an airport waiting for a delayed flight, or in your apartment when the cable's gone out.

The questions look innocent enough. At first glance, you'd never know that the cube quiz usually produces a startlingly accurate psychological profile of the person who takes it. If you're administering this quiz to a man you're fond of, be prepared to learn all sorts of inside information about his self-image, his love life, his friends, and more.

You'll need a pen and a few sheets of paper. You will do the asking while writing down answers as they're given. The cube requires a bit of creative visualization on his part and quite a lot of analytical skill on your part, as you'll be interpreting the answers and presenting your conclusions out loud at the end. Note: It's best to conduct your cube interview one on one, in a private setting.

Questions

1. You are in a desert and you see a cube.

    - How big is the cube compared to the landscape?

    - How far away is it from you?

    - What color is it?

    - What is the cube made of?

    - Is it transparent? Can you see what's inside?

2. There is also a ladder in the desert.

    - How big is the ladder?

    - Where is the ladder in relation to the cube?

    - Is it leaning on the cube?

    - What color is the ladder?

    - What is it made of?

    - About how many rungs are on the ladder?

3. There is a horse.

    - What is the distance between the cube and the horse?

    - What color is the horse?

    - How big is it?

    - Is the horse wearing a saddle, a bridle, a blanket, or anything else?

    - Describe the horse's actions.

4. There is a storm.

   – Where is the storm in relation to the cube?

   – What kind of storm is it?

   – How big is the storm in relation to the landscape?

   – Is it passing by or staying?

Answers

Here is where you must become an instant Jungian and provide a creative analysis to your subject's answers. Because there are so many possible variables, I can only provide basic guidelines; the rest is up to you. Here goes.

1. The cube represents the inner life of the person you are interviewing, and how he thinks about himself. If the cube is relatively large in relationship to the landscape, it means that his needs and feelings are important; if it is relatively small, it means that he sees himself as part of a bigger whole. If the cube is transparent, it means that he allows people in emotionally; but if it's made of glass, it could also represent emotional fragility. Hard, impenetrable materials such as steel mean that this person has built strong walls around his inner self, but strong, workable materials such as

leather or wood indicate that the person possesses both strength and flexibility.

2. The ladder represents his friends, family, and/or support system. The size of the ladder indicates how important friends and community are to him. If the ladder is leaning against the cube, it means that others depend on him; if the ladder is supporting the cube or is lying under the cube, it means that he depends on others. The distance between the cube and the ladder represents how close he feels to his tribe; and the structure, color, and material of the ladder indicates how he perceives his support system. For instance, if the ladder is made of rubber or has so few rungs that it can't be scaled, he's insecure about the reliability of his friends and family. If, on the other hand, it's a sturdy, gleaming ladder that's solidly planted on the ground, he feels secure about his inner circle.

3. The horse is his lover. If the horse is far away from the cube or off in the distance, it means that he's either not in a relationship right now or is not emotionally close to his lover. A muscular, free-galloping horse represents a sexual relationship that might not be particularly stable. Conversely, an old gray mare might indicate a relationship that is comfortable but lacks sexual excitement. If the

horse is wearing a bridle or saddle, it means that he likes to be in control of his lover. If it's wearing a blanket or something similar, he is protective without being possessive. If it's wearing nothing, he appreciates having a mate with an independent spirit. Note: If the person you're interviewing is not in a relationship, the horse he visualizes might represent the lover he'd like to have.

4. The storm represents troubles or obstacles in his life. If the storm engulfs or obscures the cube, it can mean that difficulties are presently right on top of him; it can also mean that trouble is always part of his life and that he operates under a black cloud, so to speak. If the storm is far away from the cube, it means that he doesn't allow obstacles to get in his way, but it might also indicate that he doesn't confront troubles and instead represses or ignores them. When the storm is passing through the landscape, the implication is that he's a survivor who can carry on in spite of occasional misfortunes. The intensity of the storm reflects the severity of his difficulties.

THE INTROVERT/EXTROVERT TEST

An extrovert is generally an optimistic person who responds to the stimuli of the external world and enjoys the crush of the crowd. Extroverts are often charming and usually great fun to be with, but can be somewhat shallow, choosing sensation over self-reflection or considered thought.

An introvert is one who prefers his own company, has a small and selective social life, and often takes a pessimistic view of people and events outside his window. Introverts aren't exactly party boys, but many have rich and well-developed interior lives, with a special interest in intellectual and spiritual pursuits.

So which type is your guy? One way to find out is to give him the following test, which lists twelve imaginary scenarios. Read each one to the man you're scrutinizing, and ask him if he agrees with the statement or if the described scene sounds like something he'd do. When he answers yes, mark the item with a check. When he answers no, do nothing.

__ 1. You'd rather vacation in a remote lodge than a bustling resort hotel.

__ 2. When telling a story, you sometimes embellish the details for dramatic effect.

__ 3. You go to a party at a friend's house, but it's so crowded and noisy that you leave early.

__ 4. When emergencies arise at work, you're ready and willing to drop everything and save the day.

__ 5. When traveling by train or plane, you arm yourself with books, paperwork, or a sleep mask in order to discourage your seatmate from trying to start a conversation with you.

__ 6. At home, you generally keep a TV, radio, or stereo playing in the background.

__ 7. You relish any opportunity to work alone.

__ 8. You'd rather take on short-term projects (days, weeks) than long-term projects (months, years).

__ 9. You're careful with your money.

__ 10. You'd rather be onstage than in the audience.

__ 11. Your home is your private oasis; noisy neighbors, jackhammers in the street, barking dogs, and car alarms can drive you crazy.

__ 12. You're hosting a small dinner party. One hour before it's due to start, you get a call from two friends who have just blown into town. You invite them without hesitation, even though it means you have to scrounge up extra chairs and rethink your portions.

Answer Key

If he's given the nod to mostly *even-numbered statements*, he has strong extrovert qualities. Six even numbers is a perfect score, which indicates an extreme extrovert. As a partner, this guy can be tons of fun. He craves adventure and activity, and is always willing to try new things. The extrovert is a social creature who believes that more is, indeed, merrier: He likes having lots of pals and prefers traveling in a group. Extroverted women (of varying degrees) are best matched with extroverted men (of varying degrees), because both have outgoing personalities and share a spirit of joie de vivre. If you're possessive or have a jealous streak, steer clear of high-scoring extroverts. Many are incurable flirts, and that behavior—no matter how innocent—would torment you to no end.

If most of his check marks are next to *odd-numbered answers*, he's an introvert at heart. A perfect score is six odd-numbered answers, which is the sign of a very, very introverted individual. In general, the introverted man is a quiet sort who marches to his own drummer and doesn't require the attention or the approval of strangers. Still waters run deep, however. When an introvert lets you into his private world, it's a meaningful move on his part. Once there, you might discover a multilayered reality that feeds your soul as well as your heart. If you're something of an introvert yourself, you might never want to leave. Major extroverts, on the other hand, should think twice before hooking up with an introverts. The outgoing, action-craving extrovert could very well feel stifled, unsatisfied, or oppressed by the introvert's reclusive universe.

When scores are *closely matched* between extroverted and introverted — say, four of one and five of the other — you can make your assessment by combining the above descriptions of each type, giving more weight to the high scorer.

If your subject's check marks are *equally distributed* between even numbers and odd numbers, it means that he is gifted with a large repertoire of life skills. In a perfect world, this guy is serious and silly; deep and breezy; philosophical and popular. On the other hand, he could be pessimistic and flaky; negative and shallow; antisocial and a show-off. For your sake, I hope his mix is terrific and beautifully balanced.

VACATIONS ARE FOR LOVERS

When taken as a couple, vacations can be delightful and delicious. They offer opportunity for romance and togetherness, they're a great escape from what's familiar, and they allow the two of you to work as a team in new territory. If planned well, a vacation can bring a relationship to new levels. If planned poorly, it can promote arguments, stony silences, or bitter breakups.

When shopping for a new boyfriend, consider his

taste in holiday getaways. A man's paradise can be a woman's hell, and vice versa.

This test should be taken by both of you. Check off your most honest responses, using two ink colors to differentiate between his choices and yours, then total your answers and compare them at the end.

1. Which of the following is your favorite type of vacation?

___ a. Outdoorsy adventure trips that center on hiking, water sports, horseback riding, skiing, etc.

___ b. Relaxing holidays that offer plenty of nothing to do in beautiful surroundings

___ c. Vacations spent exploring the cultural pulse of major cities, such as Paris, Rome, London, or Athens

___ d. Journeys to distant places that are unlikely to be crowded by American tourists (e.g., Santiago, Helsinki, Pretoria, Bombay, or Tasmania)

2. Your travel agent offers you four accommodations options, all in the location of your choice and in the same price range. Which do you choose?

___ a. A rustic lodge

___ b. An historic bed and breakfast

___ c. A modern hotel

___ d. A private houseboat

3. It's dinnertime. Where would you prefer to eat?

___ a. Around a roaring campfire

___ b. On the deck of a friend's bungalow

___ c. In a top-rated restaurant

___ d. At an out-of-the-way dive that serves authentic local cuisine

4. Your vacationmate is driving you crazy. Why?

___ a. He or she resists most of your suggestions

___ b. Your companion makes separate plans in order to have independent adventures

___ c. He or she insists on staying in at night and going to bed early

___ d. Your companion whines about the quality of accommodations, food, services, etc.

5. While on vacation, you're invited to use one of the following forms of transportation for one day. Which do you choose?

___ a. An all-terrain vehicle

___ b. A horse and buggy

___ c. A private compartment on a European-style train

___ d. A helium balloon

6. Of the choices below, which would you *least* enjoy doing on your vacation?

___ a. Shopping

___ b. Going to an amusement park

___ c. Taking a guided bus tour

___ d. Visiting historical re-creations (colonial villages, etc.)

7. On your way home, your connecting flight is canceled and you're stranded for eight hours. The airline is willing to offer various forms of compensation. How do you make the most of the situation?

___ a. In order to avoid waiting in the airport, you explore other transportation options — trains, buses, rental cars — and ask the airline to foot the bill

___ b. You request that the airline comp you a room in a nearby hotel so you can get some rest

___ c. You negotiate for frequent flier miles, upgrades to first class, flight vouchers, or other future-travel perks

___ d. You take the opportunity to check out the city in which you're stranded, and get the airline to pay for as much of your visit as possible

8. You've had a wonderful holiday. Which activity or event will likely be most memorable to you?

___ a. Almost losing your grip while rock climbing

___ b. Reading on the beach

___ c. Dancing all night at the hottest club in town

___ d. Getting an astonishingly accurate psychic reading from a local shaman or priestess

Scoring

Add up both of your answers by letter and record the totals below.

HIS:

a ___

b ___

c ___

d ___

YOURS:

a ___

b ___

c ___

d ___

Results

A = The Thrill-Chaser

Four or more *a* answers point to vacationers who feel most free when they're physically active in the great outdoors. Thrill-Chasers love to mix it up with Mother Nature, and often pit their strength against earth, water, and wind. If six or more of your answers are *a*, you're a true Chaser who might be drawn to cliff-diving, mountain climbing, ocean voyages in a sailboat, or other dangerous, exhilarating adventures. Thrill-Chasers travel best with their own kind, but can also have a ball with Intrepid Individualists. When paired with Peace-Seekers or Cultured Cosmopolitans, they should be prepared to balance their outdoor antics with passive diversions and understand that these types typically aren't interested in "roughing it."

B = The Peace-Seeker

B options are all about relaxation, and that is what the Peace-Seeker—who chooses at least four *b* answers—asks from a vacation. Simple pleasures such as lazy days, ambling excursions, and home-cooked meals are balms to this creature's soul. Six or more *b* answers indicate an über-Peace-Seeker who is eager to take his/her mental phone off the hook. This traveler is escaping from the demands of "real life" and values downtime more than planned activities. He or she requires privacy and might return to the same destination—say, a cottage on a beach—year after year to unwind in soothing, familiar surroundings. Peace-Seekers can settle in beautifully with like-minded Seekers, but also might be compatible with certain Intrepid Individualists. In order to get along with Thrill-Chasers or Cultured Cosmopolitans, however, Peace-Seekers should plan some alone time so that they can recharge their batteries in splendid solitude, while their eager companions conquer the world of their choice.

C = *The Cultured Cosmopolitan*

C answers (four or more) belong to those who pursue the best of everything. They crave luxury and enjoy being pampered, but their true vacation goal is to be aesthetically and intellectually stimulated. Cultured Cosmos tend to gravitate toward thriving cities, where inspiration can be found in boutiques, theatres, cafés, studios, lecture halls, clubs, and street corners. If you've made your mark on six or more *c* answers, you're probably turned on by newness and have the most fun when you can stay at the best hotel in town, snag reservations at the hottest new restaurants, attend theatre openings, discover ultra-cool nightclubs, and get invited to after-hours parties. Your ideal travelmate should have at least four *c* answers or fall slightly on the Intrepid Individualist side of life. Otherwise, you might have to answer his whims by day, then take control of the itinerary when night falls.

D = *The Intrepid Individualist*

Have you checked off at least four *d* responses? If so, you're a person who wants an authentic travel experience and is attracted to roads less traveled. Six or more *d* answers describe an extreme Intrepid Individualist who yearns to become immersed in unfamiliar surroundings. The goal is to become educated and perhaps even enlightened; as such, this type has no problem striking up conversations with interesting strangers and will gladly pursue options that others might consider way too risky (e.g., dining at the home of a new acquaintance, riding motorcycles with the locals, or venturing into neighborhoods that guidebooks advise against). If this describes you, then you'll get along famously with other Intrepid Individualists and might also find vacation harmony with certain Thrill-Chasers (as long as there are physical challenges involved). Handle Peace-Seekers and Cultured Cosmopolitans with care, however. Both types require a certain sense of control over their surroundings and might not be quite as enchanted by the idea of "going native" as you are.

YOU'RE NOT JEALOUS, ARE YOU?

Here's a revealing quiz that will gauge the jealousy level of your current amour. It's a quick and easy test, but you've got to set the stage: Ask him the questions when the two of you are relaxed and happy—you know, sitting on a park bench, heating up a pizza, or talking on the phone late at night—and check the answer of his reply. Make him promise to be totally truthful, and make sure you give it to him at a time when he's got absolutely nothing to be jealous about.

The Jealousy Quiz

1. One night at the billiard hall, you find yourself playing pool with an attractive female. The two of you flirt and banter. She beats you, and the person signed up to play her next is your best friend; they connect and end up leaving together. How do you feel?

__ a. You're disappointed but figure their attraction was stronger.

__ b. You're wounded and wonder why she picked him over you.

__ c. You're angry and feel like your best friend totally dissed you.

2. The girl of your dreams has landed a major role in an off-Broadway play — thanks, in part, to your support and encouragement. You attend the play on opening night. That's when you learn that she's playing the role of a nymphomaniac who spends most of her time onstage half-naked and humping various men. After the show, you can barely look her in the eyes because:

___ a. You thought you had helped her snag a role that featured her acting — not her boobs and thighs.

___ b. She didn't warn you that she'd be appearing seminude and performing raunchy actions. It was embarrassing — and what if you'd invited your mother?

___ c. She humiliated you and debased herself by simulating sex with a bunch of men in front of a theatre full of strangers. She might as well be a stripper.

3. During a long, intimate conversation with your new girlfriend, you learn that her ex was a Major League baseball player. This information hits you like a ton of bricks, and you:

___ a. Get excited and start pumping her for details about the players and their lifestyles.

___ b. Say nothing, but wonder how you could ever fill his shoes.

___ c. Feel threatened and start bad-mouthing the ex-boyfriend's team and professional sports in general.

4. Your younger brother announces his engagement to a wonderful woman whom you and your family are crazy about. You're still single. What are you thinking?

___ a. "Good for him. I can only hope that I'll find as great a girl someday."

__ b. "Better him than me. I'm going to make the most of my single years."

__ c. "I bet I can find someone even better between now and his wedding day."

5. Your girlfriend's ex-boyfriend invites the two of you to join a bunch of people at his beach house for a weekend of sailing. How do you R.S.V.P.?

__ a. It's a definite yes. Sounds like a blast, and you're sure you'll get along with the ex just fine.

__ b. You're nervous about going, but more afraid that your girlfriend will go by herself. You accept the invitation and hope it works out.

__ c. Absolutely not. You don't want any contact with her ex, and you'll make her promise that she won't go, either.

6. You've been an independent filmmaker for many years. You've just learned that one of your former interns, whom you took under your wing and carefully mentored, has scored an award for his first film at the Cannes Film Festival — a goal you have never been able to achieve. How do you feel?

__ a. You're proud that your little protégé has made a name for himself.

__ b. You feel twangs of pain and wonder if you should be more aggressive in promoting your own films.

__ c. You know it's irrational, but you're furious that your former ward walked away with your teachings and eclipsed your success.

7. You're having a heated discussion with an acquaintance about the merits of Macintosh computers versus PCs. In the middle of it, your computer-illiterate girlfriend walks in, takes the other guy's side, and starts defending the IBM-clone PCs. You're upset because:

__ a. She doesn't have the experience to back up her arguments and is obviously parroting something she's read or heard.

__ b. She's arguing against you, even though you're the one who sends and receives her e-mail when she needs it.

__ c. She chose the other guy's side and has formed an alliance against you.

8. It's Friday evening, and your sweetie is getting ready for a rare "girls' night out." She emerges in a sexy outfit that exposes lots of cleavage and leg — the kind of thing she rarely wears when she's out with you. What do you say?

__ a. "You look great. I can't wait for you to get home so I can ravage you."

__ b. "I'll let you get away with it this time. But next time we go out, that's what you're wearing."

___ c. "If you intend to pick up men, I'm out of here. If you don't intend to pick up men, you'd better change into something less slutty."

Scoring

a answers = 1 point
b answers = 2 points
c answers = 3 points

8–12 POINTS: He doesn't have a jealous bone in his body. Is he supremely confident? Or is he oblivious? He either deserves a pat on the back or a new prescription for his lenses.

13–19 POINTS: This midrange score implies that he's an average guy, jealousy-wise. He gets a bit anxious when his woman — or his friends — show him up, but he's rarely oppressive or irrational.

20–24 POINTS: Yikes! The green-eyed monster lives. He's not only jealous, he's also possessive, and that behavior is most definitely not what you or any woman wants. He needs to drink some chamomile tea, light a citrus candle, take a vanilla-scented bath, go into therapy — whatever it takes to chill out.

THE DALAI LAMA QUIZ

The Internet is like a giant game of telephone, in which messages are translated, retyped, and amended as they make their way around the world.

A case in point is the following personality test. According to unofficial Internet sources, it is approved by none other than the Dalai Lama, the spiritual and political leader of Buddhist Tibet. "The mind is like a parachute," quotes the nameless e-mail sage. "It works best when it is opened."

Whether this Dalai Lama Quiz has deep spiritual roots or not, it is definitely interesting and has surprising results. Take it yourself—one question at a time—then give it to your favorite fellow. You'll get a fresh new view of the inside of his head and heart.

1. Put the following animals in the order of your preference.

    cow   #_____
    tiger   #_____
    sheep   #_____
    horse   #_____
    pig   #_____

2. Write one word that describes each of the following.

dog _____

cat _____

rat _____

coffee _____

sea _____

3. Visualize each color listed below, and name a person in your life (someone who knows you and is important to you) whom you associate with that color.

yellow _____

orange _____

red _____

white _____

green _____

4. Choose your favorite day of the week. Then pick a number from 1 to 12 and write that number next to your chosen day.

Sunday #_____

Monday #_____

Tuesday #_____

Wednesday #_____

Thursday #_____

Friday #_____

Saturday #_____

Results

1. The order of these answers defines your priorities in life.

> cow — signifies career
> tiger — signifies pride
> sheep — signifies love
> horse — signifies family
> pig — signifies money

2. Here's how to interpret your one-word descriptions.

> dog — describes your own personality
> cat — describes the personality of your partner
> rat — describes your enemies
> coffee — applies to your sex life
> sea — suggests your personal potential

3. This question exposes the true colors inside your head and reveals how you think of others in non-verbal terms.

> yellow = a person who makes you uncomfortable, or whom you're in conflict with at the moment
> orange = a true friend
> red = someone you deeply love
> white = your twin soul
> green = a person you will remember forever

4. The number you picked represents a significant month in the coming year of your life. When that month comes around, pay special attention to the day of the week you chose as your own. If, for instance, your number is 3 and your day is Wednesday, then every Wednesday in March is a special time when your wishes might come true.

EMOTIONAL I.Q.

Your guy might be a Mensa candidate with an I.Q. of 162, but those brains don't mean much if he doesn't have the emotional intelligence to back them up.

In the past decade or so, standard intelligence quotient (I.Q.) tests have been attacked from all sides. One particularly devastating weapon has been the test known as E.Q. or E.-I.Q., which gauges a person's ability to interact effectively with other humans.

An official, complete emotional intelligence test includes about 70 questions and can take 40 minutes or more to complete. Here, we present E.Q. Junior, an abbreviated true-or-false test that provides a quick overview of the smarts of his heart.

T F 1. When someone experiences the death of a loved one, I reach out and offer my condolences, whether I'm close to the grieving person or not.

T F 2. I am comfortable hugging adults of either gender.

T F 3. I tend to imagine the worst possible outcome of a situation, then work hard to avoid it.

T F 4. Even when I do my best, I feel guilty about things that did not get done to my liking.

T F 5. When there is an unpleasant task at hand, I do it right away and get it over with.

T F 6. Stress, in one form or another, is always present in my life.

T F 7. I do not get angry when verbally attacked.

T F 8. It's easy for me to give compliments.

T F 9. It's easy for me to receive compliments.

T F 10. When I need to confront someone about an unpleasant issue, I try to do it in writing or over the phone rather than in person.

Scoring Key

(1) T=2, F=1; (2) T=2, F=1; (3) T=1, F=2; (4) T=1, F=2; (5) T=2, F=1; (6) T=1, F=2; (7) T=2, F=2; (8) T=2, F=1; (9) T=2, F=2; (10) T=1, F=2.

Results

A score of 18–20 indicates a high level of emotional intelligence, with 20 being a perfect score. The high-E.Q. guy has deep feelings and expresses them appropriately, but doesn't indulge himself in negativity or self-pity.

The man who scores 15–17 points is on the right path but needs to work on his communication skills. Chances are he's got good intentions but lacks experience or guidance.

A total of 12–14 points is either a sign of emotional immaturity or an ongoing stress disorder. Both can be fixed, but neither is an easy job.

THE CONTROL FREAK TEST

The following 12 questions can help separate the laid-back from the uptight. Is your guy impulsive and up for anything? Is he flexible yet sensible? Or does he micromanage his life with the frugality of Scrooge and the rigidity of Nurse Ratched?

All he has to do is answer yes or no.

Y N 1. Do you regularly contribute to a retirement fund or savings plan?

Y N 2. Does the idea of borrowing money from family members or friends seem humiliating to you?

Y N 3. If you won the lottery, would you invest 70 percent or more of your winnings?

Y N 4. Do you have a good idea of how much cash you're carrying at any given time?

Y N 5. Do you keep your car on a regular maintenance schedule?

Y N 6. Do you lay your clothes out or choose your outfit the night before?

Y N 7. Does clutter disturb or distract you?

Y N 8. Do you want to have a clean desk at day's end?

Y N 9. When making a major purchase, do you research your options and compare prices before buying?

Y N 10. If a purchase didn't meet your expectations, would you return it without hesitation?

Y N 11. When you can't find something around the house or the office, do you stop everything until the item is located?

Y N 12. Do you start planning your vacations at least four months in advance?

Answer Key

FREE AND EASY: If he answered yes to fewer than five questions, he has the ability to be adaptable and spontaneous. He's able to let go but should guard against recklessness.

RESPONSIBLE, NOT RIGID: The person who has five to eight yes answers is probably well-balanced and can take care of business without letting self-imposed rules run his life.

WHITE-KNUCKLE GRASP: More than eight yes answers point toward a disciplined creature who doesn't like surprises and uses his regimented routine as a security blanket. *Ding!* Control freak!

THE EX-SIGNIFICANT-OTHER QUIZ

So, what do you know about your current Romeo's former relationships? How much should you know? Can his past romantic liaisons shed light on your future? You'll soon find out, but take note: This test is not the kind of multiple-choice quiz you might find in a magazine. Rather, it presents a series of leading questions about his former love life and helps you to interpret his answers.

The purpose of the Ex-Significant-Other (X.S.O.) Quiz is to give you a glimpse of your potential mate's emotional landscape, based on his perceptions of the past. The key to interpretation is not in the gory details of his responses; it is in the way he handles the questions. Is he kind and decent when describing his X.S.O. and their relationship? Does he protect her privacy? Does he speak about her in a way that doesn't threaten you or make you feel inferior? Those are the gentlemanly qualities you're looking for. Of course, you also want to make sure that he's not a borderline psycho who's gnawing his way through a lifetime of serial relationships.

This quiz should only be attempted in an environment of trust. Please don't read the questions aloud, directly from the page; instead, ask them naturally in the course of open, loving conversation. Note that there are no right or wrong answers; there are only honest responses that can later be scrutinized and analyzed by you in the privacy of your own home.

Warning: Direct questions often elicit direct answers. In this case, the answers may hurt you or cause you to feel jealous. Are you willing to take that risk? If so, read on.

BEFORE YOU START: Make sure you're both talking about his most significant ex-lover. You want to discuss the person he was most serious about, whether that love match ended seven months or seven years ago.

1. How long were you two in a relationship?

__ *a. Short term (from one to six months):* Unless the fella you're (secretly) interviewing is very young — say, under 22 — this is a suspiciously short amount of time to have been with the most significant of X.S.O.s. Be sure to follow up with questions about how many relationships he's had and how long they've lasted. It could be that you're dealing with a somewhat shallow guy who is only interested in the honeymoon phase of romantic relationships.

__ *b. Long term (three years or more):* The longer

the relationship, the harder it is to recover from it, according to conventional wisdom. Be sure that plenty of time has elapsed since the ending of his long involvement—six months, at least. Otherwise, your actions will be judged in contrast to his X.S.O. Worse, you may find yourself on the wrong end of a rebound.

__ *c. Medium term (more than six months but less than three years):* Medium-term relationships are usually a good sign, because they indicate that the guy in question can make a commitment but doesn't get himself trapped in less-than-perfect situations. If his relationship length falls closer to six months, see the short-term description (above); if it falls closer to three years, see the long-term scenario.

2. What did she look like?

__ *a. "Gorgeous," "great body," "knockout," "36-26-36," etc.:* There's nothing wrong with a man having a love affair with a *Playboy*-worthy woman. But any guy who makes a big deal about the physical beauty of his ex is probably (1) completely insensitive; (2) bragging in an ass-backwards way about his own desirability; (3) immature; or (4) all of the above. This kind of response is forgivable only if he follows it up with disclaimers such as

(1) "She thought she was the center of the universe"; (2) "Her life was completely ruled by the condition of her boobs and thighs"; (3) "I find you much more attractive than her"; or (4) all of the above.

___ b. *"About five-foot-six, red hair, blue eyes, hundred twenty-five pounds . . ."*: When a man describes his ex as if he's giving a police report, it could be that he's an accuracy freak who is taking your question a little too literally. However, if his inventory includes details such as "creamy skin, a tiny dimple on her left hip, long black eyelashes," etc., it very possibly means that he's still thinking about her in a less-than-sisterly way.

___ c. *"Attractive," "fairly attractive," "great looking in her own way," etc.*: Broadly defined and vaguely complimentary definitions are the gentleman's way of describing the looks of his ex. He doesn't offend you, he doesn't insult her, and he doesn't go into detail. Perfect.

3. What caused your relationship to end?

___ a. *His dissatisfaction:* "She wanted too much," "She wasn't there for me," "Our relationship got really boring," "I wanted to move on," etc. It's a strong man who can leave a relationship that isn't working for him, no matter how comfortable or convenient it's become. However, you may want to probe a bit further — was he, in fact, neglecting her, ignoring her, even cheating on her? It's possible, and a few more gentle questions might get you the answers you need.

___ *b. Circumstances beyond his control:* "She found somebody new," "She took a job overseas and the long-distance thing didn't work for her," "I wanted to get married and she didn't," etc. Breaking up under these circumstances could mean that extreme trauma was suffered by the male. He might still be harboring unresolved feelings toward his X.S.O., so be on the lookout.

___ *c. Mutual dissatisfaction:* "We grew apart," "We wanted different things," "We just couldn't get along any more," etc. This is the most gentlemanly way to describe a relationship's demise: no blame, no anger, no lurid details. Of course, we all know that there's no such thing as a pretty end to a love affair, but mutually agreed upon breakups are the kindest and most mature of them all.

4. Was your breakup painful?

___ *a. No:* "Not really," "Not for me," etc. Of course, this is a trick question — virtually all breakups are painful. The man who masks that fact may very well be in denial about a deep sense of mourning or regret. Did he behave badly in his relationship? Did he storm out without explanation? Did he jump from one relationship to another without looking back? Did she hurt him so badly that he completely shut down? Or did he genuinely not care anymore? You may want to investigate these possibilities further.

__ *b. Yes:* "It was terrible," "I fell to pieces," "It took me years to get over her," etc. When a man admits to being in emotional pain — even if he answers with a simple yes — you can bet it was excruciating. You can also be pretty sure that it left a scar. It is up to you to intuit how much healing has gone on. Is he still angry and hurt? Is he still pining over her? Or is he ready to open himself to another relationship? The fact that he acknowledges his own pain is a promising sign.

__ *c. I guess so:* "It was tough at first," "Yeah, but I'm totally over it," "It seems like ancient history," etc. The guy who remembers painful times but puts them in the past is probably the most emotionally healthy of the bunch. Chances are that he's gone through a complete healing process, has worked through his feelings, and his once-significant relationship truly is ancient history.

5. Are you still in touch with her?

__ *a. Absolutely not:* "Never," "Perish the thought," "I haven't spoken to her since the day we broke up," etc. Either this guy abruptly walked out on his relationship or he was brutally dumped (or his ex-girlfriend ran screaming from him). It's normal to have at least a bit of communication after a breakup; it's normal to run into an ex once in awhile and exchange small talk; it's also normal, after a period of time or distance, to never see or hear from an ex. But an instant and absolute shut-off of all communication smacks of anger, hostility, and/or guilt. Unless his ex was a crazy woman who stalked or tormented him, you should be suspicious of a man who won't be civil toward the former love of his life.

__ *b. Absolutely yes:* "We're best of friends," "I see her all the time," "I'm the godfather of her child," etc. There's nothing technically wrong with a man remaining close with his X.S.O. It can be kind of nice, in fact. But how close is too close? Is he unable or unwilling to make an emotional break from her? Even if he is, do you really want his ex in the background of your future relationship, bearing witness to your every move? You might end up in an unpleasant situation in which you're forced to ask him to choose between her and you.

__ c. *Sort of:* "Our paths cross now and then," "We exchange Christmas cards," "I run into her at the supermarket," etc. A comfortable, polite distance is the best-case scenario when it comes to dealing with former lovemates. It's admirable when a man can keep the past in the past, stay free of grudges, and behave gracefully, even when awkward situations arise.

Scoring

The man with mostly *a* answers is probably standing on shaky ground, emotionwise. His actions speak louder than his words; he might be a poor communicator who gets by on the "strong, silent type" image, or he might be a charming sweet-talker who says all the right things in order to get his way. In any case, he is likely a person who avoids real emotional intimacy. Even if he's not Mr. Right, he might be Mr. Right Now. Just remember to look before you leap.

Mostly *b* answers indicate a guy who is very much in touch with his feelings, but who carries a lot of emotional baggage. Though he probably has no problem with intimacy, he may have a deep fear of commitment due to painful past experiences. If you choose this man, remember that he feels safe in friendship but is worried by love. Proceed one step at a time and be prepared for a long, slow, gentle courtship.

The more *c* answers, the better the prospect. These responses point toward a man who feels safe in his own skin and who takes responsibility for his actions. Emotionally mature, he is able to give and take in equal measure and has the capacity to be sensitive, flexible, and respectful without being a doormat. Best of all, he's gentlemanly in word and deed.

ARE YOU THE TRUSTING TYPE?

Some people are trusting by nature and put their faith in fate, good karma, and the basic decency of humankind. On the opposite end of the spectrum are cautious folk, who look before they leap. Their instincts tell them to make investigations, explore options and possibilities, and arm themselves against worst-case scenarios.

In relationship land, trust is an unspoken contract between two individuals, and the sanctity of that bond is essential to the health of both parties. Some people trust more easily than others, however. And that's what this quiz is all about.

Snag some quiet time with your loved one—in the hot tub, on the beach, after breakfast on a lazy Sunday—and take this quiz together. These eight yes-or-no questions will teach you about each other's baseline tolerance for risk. Which one of you plays it safe, and which one goes by blind faith? A greater understanding of each other's basic instincts can help strengthen your bond.

Y N 1. Your sweetheart of two months is running some errands for you. Do you hand over your credit card and let him/her sign your name for the purchases?

Y N 2. Do you often pay restaurant bills without checking them?

Y N 3. Would you consider an overseas house-swap, in which a foreign couple you've never met stayed in your place for two weeks, while you stayed in theirs?

Y N 4. Your mate's long-ago ex thinks it would be fun if the two of them attended this year's high school reunion together. Do you allow it?

Y N 5. You're having new flooring installed in your bedroom. Do you let the installers do their work when you're not home?

Y N 6. A friend asks to borrow your car. He promises he'll have it back by 6:00 P.M.; you urgently need it no later than 6:30 P.M. in order to make a flight. Do you take a chance and let him have it?

Y N 7. Do you purchase items off the Internet?

Y N 8. While gathering up clothes to be dry-cleaned, you find a cocktail napkin in your mate's jacket pocket. Scrawled on it are a phone number and the words CALL ME! You toss it in the garbage and let it slide.

Scoring

You guessed it: The more *yes* answers you have, the more trusting you are. There's a fine line between trust and recklessness, however. People who have *seven or eight yes answers* may feel carefree, but suspicious types see that type of behavior as careless and fraught with unnecessary risks. This more trusting person should avoid getting involved with extremely cautious types.

If *five or six of your answers were yes*, it means you have your feet on the ground, yet still have faith in human nature. This is a nice balance. You are a trusting person with a healthy handle on reality, and you easily capture and hold the trust of virtually all other types.

Four or five no responses indicate a person who proceeds with caution but is willing to take a good-faith risk now and then. This type matches up well with more trusting souls and can lend a voice of reason without squashing the other's spirit.

If you've said *no to six or more questions*, your trust thermometer registers between reasonably suspicious (six to seven) and very suspicious (eight). You make decisions with your head, not your heart, and do your best to keep disaster, failure, and heartache at bay. Find your best mate among the midrange of trusting types, who will recognize your approach to life as intelligent, rather than cynical.

"WELL, I NEVER!"

Beware: This party game can be shocking, strange, and wildly revealing. It's best played between four to eight people who like and trust each other, don't know everything about each other's personal lives, and don't have heart conditions.

If you want to coax secrets and confessions out of the guy you desire, this is the game for you. With each passing round, he'll be forced to dig ever deeper into his private vault to unearth fascinating truths about himself and say them out loud. How delicious.

The rules are easy. Taking turns around the room, the player who is "it" names something that he or she has never done. If everybody else in the room has done that thing, the player earns one point and takes another turn. If one or more players have also never done that thing, no points are earned and the game moves on to the next person.

Example: Let's say that Barbara goes first and tells the group that she's never had a cavity. If Steve announces that he's never had a cavity either, Barbara gets nothing. If, on the other hand, everybody in the room has had a cavity, Barbara scores a point.

The first person to earn five points wins.

Sounds simple, but, as the game progresses, the confessions get more intimate and astounding. True story: During one particularly lively game, a successful actor friend announced that he'd never graduated from high school. Everybody was shocked—then doubly shocked when another player, who owns a thriving business, admitted that he'd never graduated from high school either. The brave actor didn't even earn a point for his painful confession.

To get you started, here are some interesting "nevers." Perhaps you, your friends, or your boy du jour have never: eaten a clam . . . broken a bone . . . gotten a ticket . . . dated outside of your race or religion . . . been to a strip club . . . had surgery . . . cheated on anyone . . . gone fishing . . . been to Vegas . . . smoked a cigarette . . . had a one-night stand . . . been on skis . . . owned a cat . . . been to a football game . . . gone without underwear . . . eaten with chopsticks . . . seen a dead body . . . been on a blind date . . . seen *The Godfather* . . . traveled outside of the country . . . been in love.

Does He Fit? Find Your Compatibility Factor

You've examined him under your personal microscope. You've given him emotional X-rays and ardent MRIs. Now it's time to find out whether the man you want is the man you need.

Will you and he get along in the long run? It's a big question that has been asked for centuries. Certain ancient systems—especially those based on astrology—allege that compatibility is determined by dates of birth. Some modern systems, on the other hand, maintain that successful couplehood is based on sympathetic personality traits.

Dive bravely into Chapter Three and see how the two of you rate as long-term lovers.

YOUR ASTROLOGICAL MATCHMAKER

Good old astrology. It's been around forever, but never gets old. It's delivered fresh every morning in the daily papers and on personal home pages; we eagerly read our horoscopes in the back of glossy magazines and listen with hot ears to recorded messages that have something to say about our immediate future.

Astrology was once considered to be a serious science, did you know? That was before the dawn of the sixteenth century, when Copernicus decided that Earth does not occupy a fixed position in space. Since that time, the zodiac has been more about human nature and less about heavenly bodies. And we the people have embraced its teachings and forecasts. Everybody wants to be a child of the universe, now and forever.

You already know a thing or two about your sign, right? Good. We'll skip the in-depth analysis and go directly to the boy-crazy stuff.

Your mission:

1. Locate your astrological sign below.
2. Read the accompanying text.
3. Discover where in the zodiac you might find the love of your life.
4. Go get him.
5. Thank your lucky stars.

Aries
(March 21–April 19)

Sure, you're fiery and impulsive, but you just might find yourself in a desirous relationship with a Gemini, who loves to talk and can call the sensual shots; a Leo, whose powerful personality complements yours; a Scorpion, as long you as you don't make him jealous; a Sagittarian, who entertains you and challenges your mind; a Capricorn, who is as honest and hard working as you; an Aquarian, whose dreamy ways are counterbalanced by your take-charge attitude; or a Piscean, who doesn't mind being bossed around.

Taurus
(April 20–May 20)

Shopping for a perfect fit? Start by narrowing your search to the sign of Cancer, where you might find a Crab who loves your bullish power; then Virgo, where a certain someone is probably waiting to be de-prudified by you; move on to Capricorn, where you'll find candidates who adore your quiet, sexy strength; and finally Pisces, where you'll likely locate someone who appreciates (and needs) your no-nonsense approach to life.

Gemini
(May 21–June 21)

Gemini—the sign of the Twins—is a jumble of contradictions, but that doesn't mean your good man is hard to find. You click madly with the Aries male, forming a match that is all talk and all action. With Leo the Lion, a bit of compromise yields tons of potential; with Libra the Scales, you'll find peace in the parlor and fun in the bedroom. The Aquarius man is your best prospect of all, offering stimulation that ranges from intellectual to erotic.

Cancer
(June 22–July 22)

Dear Ms. Crab: Drop your defenses and take aim. Your ideal targets are men born under the sign of Taurus, who could offer long-term romance; Leo, who are sexy and true blue; Virgo, who want to please you; Scorpio, who spark with your energy in a most excellent way; and Pisces, with whom you just might find lasting trust and true love.

Leo
(July 23–August 22)

If you can stand to share the spotlight, you'll have a thrilling time with Aries dreamboats. You can go wild with a Gemini, as long as he can curb his tendency to fool around. You might find happiness with a Libran, if the two of you can control your spending habits; and you can make passionate music with a Sagittarian, if you keep him ever showered with attention. Leos and Cancers might possibly make you purr, as well.

Virgo
(August 23–September 22)

If you're like most Virgos, you believe that love and sex are equally sacred. As such, your heavenly hookup is the Taurus man, who moves you in all the right ways. But don't overlook the Libran, who can give with his whole heart and soul; Scorpions, who hold the keys to excitement and joy; and Capricorns, whose initial shyness gives way to all the intensity you could possibly handle.

Libra
(September 23–October 23)

The sages say that a Gemini can put you on cloud nine, because he enjoys beauty and pleasure almost as much as you do. Leos will shower you with love, affection, and gifts; Sagittarians will show you a great time and quench your thirst for adventure; and Aquarians are possibly your best match of all, as a man born under this sign can be both a lover and a friend, providing a magical meeting of the minds and the bodies.

Scorpio
(October 24–November 21)

As the steamiest sign of the zodiac, you're always in danger of having purely physical liaisons. Cancers can put the give-and-take into a relationship; Capricorns might lend stability and balance to the Scorpion's life; and Pisceans have all the ingredients for forging strong emotional bonds. Your best chance for lasting love is with a Virgoan, who will use his powers to keep you happy and fascinated.

Sagittarius
(November 22–December 21)

You're a wild child caught between a yearning for permanent love and a need for adventure. Never fear: Satisfying romance can be found with a spicy Arian, a laid-back Libran, or an imaginative Aquarian. But wait, there's more: For long-term relationships that will never know a dull moment, the combination of Sagittarius and Leo can't be beat.

Capricorn
(December 22–January 19)

Achievement and amour are both important to you, a Capricorn goat-girl. So you'll be glad to know that when you get together with a Taurean, there is love and money afoot. Virgos offer chemistry and stability; Scorpions bring intimacy and excitement; and the Pisces mate provides plenty of affection while helping make your dreams come true.

Aquarius
(January 20–February 18)

You water-bearers make up your own rules as you go along, which can be tough for certain signs to handle. Your best love matches are Geminis, with whom you can have loads of fun on social, romantic, and physical levels; Librans, who are flexible and accepting of your ways; Sagittarians, who share your interest in travel and philosophy; Arians, in an opposites-attract sort of way; and other Aquarians, who understand your need for a long leash and aren't prone to jealousy.

Pisces
(February 19–March 20)

Cancer the crab is a terrific partner for Pisces, as you both love staying at home and find each other's company irresistible. Other zodiac-approved candidates include the Arian (if he can curb his temper), Taurean (if he can loosen up a bit), and the Capricorn (if he doesn't indulge his dark side); but your most promising choice is a Scorpio man, whose sign is a natural match for Pisces and who doesn't require any special adjustments or compromises.

CHINESE ASTROLOGY

What is the animal that hides in his heart? Chinese astrologers can give you the answer and explain its meaning. It's all a matter of finding his birth year on the following chart, then reading the revealing results. If the year you are looking for is not in the list below, simply add or subtract 12 to the year to match it to the appropriate animal.

Rat: 1924, 1936, 1948, 1960, 1972, 1984, 1996

Ox: 1925, 1937, 1949, 1961, 1973, 1985, 1997

Tiger: 1926, 1938, 1950, 1962, 1974, 1986, 1998

Rabbit: 1927, 1939, 1951, 1963, 1975, 1987, 1999

Dragon: 1928, 1940, 1952, 1964, 1976, 1988, 2000

Snake: 1929, 1941, 1953, 1965, 1977, 1989

Horse: 1930, 1942, 1954, 1966, 1978, 1990

Sheep: 1931, 1943, 1955, 1967, 1979, 1991

Monkey: 1932, 1944, 1956, 1968, 1980, 1992

Rooster: 1921, 1933, 1945, 1957, 1969, 1981, 1993

Dog: 1922, 1934, 1946, 1958, 1970, 1982, 1994

Boar: 1923, 1935, 1947, 1959, 1971, 1983, 1995

If He's a Rat . . .

He's devilishly charming as well as aggressive, clever, talkative, quick witted, honest, and organized. His top five matches are the Dragon, Monkey, Ox, Rat, and Boar.

If He's an Ox . . .

He's a diligent, hardworking guy. On a more intimate level, he's observant, patient, caring, and loyal. Best matches for the Ox are the Rat, Rooster, Snake, Monkey, and Rabbit.

If He's a Tiger . . .

He's a born leader and is confident, independent, and fearless, yet can also be calm and sensitive. The love of his life is probably a Dog, Horse, Monkey, Boar, or Dragon.

If He's a Rabbit . . .

He's artistic, tasteful, delicate, sweet, caring, diplomatic, prudent, honest, and happy. He is most compatible with the Boar, Dragon, Sheep, Dog, and Monkey.

If He's a Dragon . . .

He's an energetic leader and is likely to be ideal-istic, professional, aggressive, and dynamic, as well as generous and intelligent. The Rat, Boar, Rabbit, Monkey, and Tiger are his designated soul mates.

If He's a Snake . . .

He's wise, intuitive, elegant, reflective, intelligent, and romantic, and tends to be on the quiet side. When looking for love, he should choose among the Rooster, Ox, Horse, Sheep, and Dog.

If He's a Horse . . .

He's quick witted, sexy, energetic, enterprising, and proud, as well as loyal, tolerant, and cheerful. Horses should set their sights on the Dog, Tiger, Sheep, Snake, and Boar.

If He's a Sheep . . .

He's gentle, kind-hearted, compassionate, adaptable, peaceful, creative, and, best of all, lucky. His best romantic matches are the Boar, Rabbit, Horse, Dragon, and Monkey.

If He's a Monkey . . .

He's lively, amusing, shrewd, observant, analytical, loyal, and passionate. He'll find his perfect mate among Rats, Monkeys, Dragons, Tigers, and Boars.

If He's a Rooster . . .

He's colorful, creative, sociable, multitalented, bold, sincere, and straightforward, with lots of stamina. He's most likely to form a happy relationship with the Snake, Ox, Boar, Monkey, or perhaps the Dragon.

If He's a Dog . . .

He's honest, faithful, dependable, tolerant, unpretentious, hardworking, helpful, and intelligent. For best romantic results, he should sniff out Horses, Tigers, Boars, Rabbits, and Rats.

If He's a Boar . . .

He's gentle, lively, gallant, impulsive, courageous, generous, obliging, sincere, and perhaps even intellectual. The love of his life is probably a Sheep, Dragon, Boar, Rabbit, or Rat.

FIND THE OPTIMIST

One of the most important qualities to look for in a potential mate is cheerfulness. It's an underrated trait and doesn't seem to find its way into compatibility quizzes in women's magazines. But cheerfulness and optimism are crucial in relationships. Few things are more depressing than being hooked up with a man who only sees flaws, glitches, mistakes, and potential disasters. It's bad enough that pessimists lack a sense of wonder (or won't allow themselves to experience wonderment); what's worse is that no matter how much you love them or how much they love you, you cannot and will not make them happy. More accurately, you will not make them cheerful. Gloom will rule. Sure, joy might pierce through the gray vapors now and then, but those moments won't last. True pessimists don't trust joy and treat it like an indulgence—an ice cream cone on a summer night, a deluxe car wash before a wedding. Then it's back to terra firma, that safe, dull place where disappointment doesn't have a chance.

Thank heaven for optimists, who keep their arms wide open and are ready to accept whatever miraculous things the universe might throw their way. Joy is what they aspire to: Though they might be deflated or even devastated, they eventually return to a hope-ful, positive state of mind. They sing in traffic jams. They turn bad experiences into amusing anecdotes. They give great pep talks. And, nine hours out of ten, they're emotionally available.

So, which is he? Give him the following quiz (they're all yes-or-no answers) and shed some light on the subject.

Y N 1. Do you enjoy celebrating milestone birth-days — 20, 30, 40, etc.?

Y N 2. Do you sometimes spend money you don't really have, just so you can participate in a wonderful experience or event?

Y N 3. Have you ever taken a trip without any plan as to where you'll stay?

Y N 4. Do you like to gamble or play games of chance?

Y N 5. Are minor disasters — temporary blackouts, fruit avalanches in the produce aisle, a bat flap-ping through the living room — exciting and fun for you?

Y N 6. If you're having a magical evening, will you stay up way past your bedtime to keep it going, even if it guarantees you'll be exhausted the next day?

Y N 7. Do you find it difficult to give up on bad relationships, lousy jobs, crummy friends, etc., unless there is a replacement already lined up?

Y N 8. Do you strive to remain on good terms with people?

Y N 9. When the gas tank is almost empty, do you prefer to think of it as one-eighth full?

Y N 10. Do you devise ways to make boring tasks more interesting?

Y N 11. Can little things (buying a cool pair of shoes, waking up to the smell of bacon, fitting a letter perfectly on a page, etc.) make you feel inordinately blissful?

Y N 12. Do you believe that your ship will eventually come in?

Answer Key

- If he's said yes to nine or more questions, he's a true optimist. Hopefully, he'll spread his cheer without compromising common sense and basic survival skills.

- The man with five to eight yes answers has a positive attitude but doesn't wear the rose-colored glasses full-time. He might embrace a "hope for the best, prepare for the worst" strategy.

- Four yes responses: negativity lurks.
- Three: pessimism creeps in.
- Two: the gloom clouds gather.
- One: cheer is smothered to death.

- Zero: in space, it's known as a black hole; on earth, it's called the über-pessimist. Unless you're a hard-core Goth chick, this guy isn't for you.

BIRTH ORDER AND HOW TO WORK IT

Psychologists make their living by studying family dynamics and making astute observations about them from a safe distance. Their scientific snooping has, among other things, resulted in a neat little system that assigns certain personality and behavioral traits to firstborn, middle-born, last-born, and only children. The system has also produced its own bastard child: Birth Order Relating, which forecasts people's compatibility based on their respective birth orders.

Once you've scoped out the details of your future husband's family, the rest is easy. You may even find out that he's not your future husband, after all.

Understanding the
Four Basic Birth Orders

ONLY CHILDREN set goals for themselves and constantly strive to meet them. Most are close with their parents and comfortable being the center of attention, but are not particularly social in general. Only children have high standards for themselves and others. Though they may be well-mannered, attentive, and perfectly polite, they aren't necessarily forgiving of those who don't make the grade.

FIRSTBORNS learn responsibility at an early age. With that lesson comes independence, self-direction, and excellent survival skills. Respect is important to firstborns, and they work hard to earn and keep it. Though loyal and doggedly honest, they're also ambitious and tenacious, and don't want anything—or anyone—to get in their way.

MIDDLE-BORNS are natural mediators. Most are open-minded and sympathetic, and can make most anyone feel comfortable. In the interest of being helpful and constructive, some can become chronically critical. Middle children tend to avoid the spotlight, preferring to work behind the scenes. They don't feel the need to make bold moves or to publicly assert themselves, and this behavior can be perceived by others as weakness or insecurity.

LAST-BORNS seek a life of adventure and excitement. Creative, fun-loving, risk-taking, and entertaining, they often have complicated social lives and unpredictable career paths. As the youngest member of the family, the last-born child is at risk of growing up to be an irresponsible adult who tries to get by on charm.

How the Birth Orders Get Along

If you're an *only child* and your beloved is . . .

- **AN ONLY CHILD:** This mix can work if the two of you are willing to live in separate worlds together and maintain a quiet understanding of each other's needs, without pressure or drama.

- **A FIRSTBORN:** Both of you are independent, take-charge types, but it is the firstborn who needs to be the alpha dog. Can you let somebody else do the driving? If so, go for it.

- **A MIDDLE-BORN:** This coupling has a fairly high rate of success. The middle-born mate can be an empathetic and supportive partner, as long as he receives plenty of affection and appreciation in return.

- **A LAST-BORN:** Somebody has to be the grown-up. In this case, it's you. With a last-born at your side, you'll never be bored, but you might be stuck with boring tasks like holding down a job and paying the bills. Beware: The "mommy role" isn't exactly sexy and can ultimately lead to the death of romance.

If you're a *firstborn* and you have your eye on . . .

- **AN ONLY CHILD:** You're bossy; he's selfish. Power struggles are practically guaranteed, but with the right combination of love and communication, you two hardheads could make a great couple.

- **A FIRSTBORN:** When two pit bulls are thrown together, they can end up with bloody gashes and broken teeth. Or, they can end up being new best friends and having a litter of pups. So it is with the firstborn plus firstborn combo: The results will be either disastrous or delightful.

- **A MIDDLE-BORN:** You two are naturally compatible, at least in theory. Success depends on your man's willingness to be patient, loving, and supportive while you're out conquering the world.

- **A LAST-BORN:** You wear the pants; he takes them off. You're a powerhouse; he's a boy toy. Or something like that. This is a rather unconventional pairing of ambitious female and free-spirited male, but it could prove to be an absolute blast for both of you.

If you're a *middle-born* and you're dreaming about . . .

- **AN ONLY CHILD:** He might bask in the glow of your friends and family, and pick up a few pointers about giving and receiving. If you choose this man, be prepared to allow him plenty of alone time.

- **A FIRSTBORN:** You'll likely find comfort in his stability and strength, just as he'll appreciate your winning way with people and problems. A fine match.

- **A MIDDLE-BORN:** Where passive meets passive, there is kindness, comfort, and understanding, but very little action. This coupling could result in stagnancy or even codependency.

- **A LAST-BORN:** As a middle-born, you can only feel secure in a completely monogamous relationship. The typical last-born is outgoing and engaging, and his flirty behavior will no doubt rattle your trust. Whether he's true to you or not, you'll probably make each other miserable.

If you're a *last-born* with a yearning for . . .

- **AN ONLY CHILD:** Make room for Daddy. This match could be healthy and happy, as long as your only-child mate enjoys, appreciates, and indulges you, while setting limits that preserve his sanity.

- **A FIRSTBORN:** You've seen the movie: High-spirited girl meets older, uptight man and melts his frozen heart. Think *Pretty Woman, My Fair Lady, Gigi, The Sound of Music* . . . the list goes on and on. If you're tempted to pursue a firstborn, remember that the men in these movies were rich, power-ful, or both. Hint, hint.

- **A MIDDLE-BORN:** This coupling has tons of potential and gets its strength from a combination of practicality (him), flexibility (him), reliability (him), and adventurousness (you).

- **A LAST-BORN:** It will be a wild ride, but will it last? Don't think about that right now. Just jump right in and enjoy being half of a dynamic duo. You never know—it might withstand the test of time.

INELIGIBLE AT ANY SPEED

According to the Universal Dating Regulations and Bylaws put forth by the American Dating Association (ADA), potential partners may not be deemed unworthy on the basis of occupation, class, or income level.

The ADA does name a few occupations and life choices that disqualify men from the dating game, however. For instance, the ADA's laws decree a man ineligible if he's an ordained Roman Catholic priest, a drug dealer, an inmate, or a hermit.

Inspired by the ADA's blacklist, I've come up with my own collection of undesirable attributes.

Your job is to go through the list and check off the various crimes of which your man is guilty. Then read the results at the end to determine whether he's worthy.

___ He's appeared as a guest on *The Jerry Springer Show, Sally Jessy Raphael Show, Montel Williams Show,* or other lowbrow TV programs. (F)

___ He's been in the studio audience of *The Jerry Springer Show, Sally Jessy Raphael Show, Montel Williams Show,* or other trash TV programs. (M)

___ His driver's license was revoked within the last five years. (M)

___ He's had a restraining order filed against him. (F)

___ He's over twenty-five and still lives with his parent(s). (M)

___ He lives more than an hour away from you. (M)

___ His job requires him to travel extensively, often, or at short notice. (M)

___ Getting drunk or high is a favorite form of recreation to him. (F)

___ He has a collection of porn (magazines, videos, downloads, etc.) (M)

___ He has a collection of extremely perverted or violent-themed porn. (F)

___ He's bisexual, and you're not. (F)

___ His place is usually a mess. (M)

__ He's almost always late. (M)

__ He can't seem to keep a job longer than six months. (M)

__ He's often short on cash. (M)

__ He has children out of wedlock. (M)

__ He has children out of wedlock and doesn't pay child support. (F)

__ He's married. (F)

Results

See those little letters at the end of each question? Add them up.

M stands for "misdemeanor." Your gentleman friend is allowed a maximum of three misdemeanors; more than that, and he's considered unseemly and unacceptable — an ineligible bachelor.

F stands for "felony." If you've checked off even one felony entry, you're dealing with a bad man. He may not be rotten to the core, but he is certainly a poor candidate for your precious love and attention. All F marks point to heartbreak and wasted time.

If he's guilt-free — or has, say, one or two misdemeanors to his name — the man in question has been cleared for takeoff. This doesn't mean he's perfect, but it does mean he's not hobbled by obvious flaws.

THE ELEMENTAL TYPES

The Eastern discipline of elemental type reading is based on birth years and assesses not only the character of each type but how well different elemental types get along. The true art of elemental type reading involves many complicated aspects, including the harmony and/or discord of yin and yang years. We've simplified it here to make it easy for beginners.

Birth Years and Their Corresponding Elemental Types

Wood

1924—25	1964—65
1934—35	1974—75
1944—45	1984—85
1954—55	1994—95

Fire

1926—27	1966—67
1936—37	1976—77
1946—47	1986—87
1956—57	1996—97

Earth

1928—29   1968—69

1938—39   1978—79

1948—49   1988—89

1958—59   1998—99

Metal

1930—31	1970—71
1940—41	1980—81
1950—51	1990—91
1960—61	2000—2001

Water

1932—33	1972—73
1942—43	1982—83
1952—53	1992—93
1962—63	2002—2003

What the Types Mean

Wood indicates a nature that is generous, self-confident, dignified, harmonious, and compassionate. Wood types are adaptive, independent, and energetic, yet have a tendency to take on more than can be managed and have a temper that can be difficult to control. They need freedom and movement in their lives and have a passion for growth, expansion, beauty, and awakening.

The Wood Woman's Compatibility Guide

- Wood man = hostile
- Fire man = nonconflicting

- Earth man = highly compatible
- Metal man = nonconflicting
- Water man = harmonious

Fire is the sign of a warm, brilliant, intuitive, and decisive nature. Fire characters are innovative, adventurous, and creative, yet their passionate nature can sometimes lead to self-destructiveness. Though they can be negative and sharp-tongued, Fire people are more often joyful, exciting, charismatic, entertaining, and magical.

The Fire Woman's Compatibility Guide

- Wood man = nonconflicting
- Fire man = nonconflicting
- Earth man = harmonious
- Metal man = unsympathetic
- Water man = hostile

Earth indicates a nature that is responsible, practical, honest, disciplined, and hardworking. Sometimes Earth characters lack a sense of romance or adventure, but they are balanced, stable, and solid, with a talent for nurturing others and sustaining a peaceful life.

The Earth Woman's Compatibility Guide

- Wood man = hostile
- Fire man = harmonious
- Earth man = harmonious
- Metal man = highly compatible
- Water man = unsympathetic

Metal indicates an energetic, active, and ambitious nature. Metal types can sustain actions and efforts with a tireless persistence, but might become rigid and inflexible to the point where it's difficult for them to relax. They tend to be both outgoing and independent, and are usually highly dependable.

The Metal Woman's Compatibility Guide

- Wood man = nonconflicting
- Fire man = hostile
- Earth man = unsympathetic
- Metal man = hostile
- Water man = highly compatible

Water is the sign of a receptive, flowing, communicative, passive, calm, and flexible nature. Water types can be persuasive and wise, but can be judgmental, become overly sensitive to others, and fail to take care of their own needs. The most psychic of the elemental types, Water people are often on a philosophical or spiritual quest for knowledge.

The Water Woman's Compatibility Guide

- Wood man = harmonious
- Fire man = hostile
- Earth man = unsympathetic
- Metal man = highly compatible
- Water man = nonconflicting

IS HE, UM, THRIFTY?

Cheap is such a cheap word, don't you think? When applied to men, it suggests a fellow who cares more about his finances than his love life. Yet each human being has distinct beliefs about money — how it should be made, spent, saved, and invested. In order to form a happy, long-lasting relationship, it is extremely important that men and women have compatible financial personalities.

If you can comfortably get your man to consider the following checklist, go for it. Otherwise, you'll have to fill in the blanks using your own best guesses. At the end of it all, you'll acquire a portfolio filled with information about his very personal investments.

His Financial Profile

Make a check mark next to each "yes" answer.

__ 1. You routinely spend money on clothes, grooming products, tanning, trainers, gym memberships, and the like.

__ 2. You avoid using alien ATM machines that charge a dollar or more for transactions.

__ 3. When out on a date, you insist on paying for everything, even if you can't really afford it.

__ 4. You feel victorious when mistakes are made in your favor (e.g., the cashier accidentally hands you an extra twenty dollars in change; the train conductor never collects your ticket; or your new apartment has an illegal cable hookup).

__ 5. It's important to you to have up-to-date electronic equipment.

__ 6. When ordering from a menu, you go for value instead of what you really want.

__ 7. When a friend, loved one, or family member is in dire financial straits, you contribute whatever you can, with no strings attached.

__ 8. At some point in your life, you've carried a hundred dollar bill as an ad hoc savings plan, figuring the bill would be difficult to spend casually.

__ 9. When a person on the street asks you for spare change, you hand over a buck or two whenever possible.

__ 10. You resent the markup on roses on Valentine's Day.

Scoring

Four or more even-numbered answers indicate a man with thrifty tendencies. Though he may not be cheap, he keeps a careful watch on his money and doesn't spend impulsively.

Four or more odd-numbered answers belong to a man with open pockets. His generosity is admirable; however, he may have an unrealistic attitude toward money that could lead to financial disaster.

The man who has a *close balance between odd- and even-numbered answers* demonstrates an ideal combination of caution and compassion. He is neither a miser nor a spendthrift, which makes him the Type O of financial personalities.

WHAT MAKES HIM LAUGH?

The sense of humor is a true window to the soul. Laughter is where the brain and the body collide, and it is a power beyond our control. We might as well try to repress a sneezing fit. Sure, we could muffle our guffaws (which is sometimes a good idea, especially in church or at a poetry reading), but there's no way to iron out that convoluted face or settle those quaking shoulders. Besides, who wants to?

It's great when you and your love share a sense of humor. Not only do you laugh at the same things, you're also able to make each other laugh.

Personality experts divide senses of humor—and the funny bones that go with them—into four basic categories. Put a check mark next to the following jokes and quips that push your laugh button. Then give the quiz to the guy who makes you smile, and see how you two match up.

__ 1. Two aunts are visiting their young niece. "Too bad she isn't c-u-t-e," one aunt whispers to the other. The girl looks up and says, "Well, at least I'm not s-t-u-p-i-d."

__ 2. Why do bagpipers walk when they play? *To get away from the sound.*

__ 3. Sex is hereditary. If your parents didn't have it, chances are you won't either.

__ 4. A duck walks into a drugstore and says, "I'd like a tube of lip balm, please. And would you put it on my bill?"

__ 5. I'd rather have a bottle in front of me than a frontal lobotomy.

__ 6. Why did God invent women? *'Cause sheep can't cook.* Why did God invent men? *'Cause vibrators can't mow the lawn.*

__ 7. A conservative is someone who believes that nothing should be done for the first time.

__ 8. What did the elephant say to the naked man? *I don't know how you can breathe through that little thing.*

__ 9. Why do Baptists object to fornication? *They're afraid it might lead to dancing.*

__ 10. The Buddha goes to a hot dog stand and says, "Make me one with everything."

__ 11. What is the difference between erotic and perverted? *Erotic is when you use a feather. Perverted is when you use the whole chicken.*

__ 12. Definition of a gentleman: a man who knows how to play the harmonica, but doesn't.

Answer Key

If you liked jokes number 1, 7, and 9 you tend toward the *satirical*. This sense of humor usually belongs to a fairly sophisticated person who is well informed and notices the foibles of human behavior.

Were 2, 8, and 12 your favorites? Then *aggressive* humor is what appeals to you. Though it's not outwardly mean, this brand of comedy takes negative (some would say realistic) observations and wraps them in a neutralizing layer of laughs.

If 3, 6, and 11 were funniest to you, then you're drawn to *sexual* humor. Chances are you're an outgoing person who enjoys jokes in general, but who is especially tickled by risqué or taboo subjects.

Jokes number 4, 5, and 10 fall into the *absurdist* camp. Did the duck, bottle, and Buddha grab you? Then you're likely a literate person who appreciates clever wordplay and prefers humor that isn't shocking or offensive.

Compatibility Key

Your best match is the guy who laughs at the same jokes that you do. If the two of you share the same humor category, that's a very good sign. Not so lucky? Here are other promising combinations:

- Aggressive jokesters tend to get along with those who enjoy sexual humor.

- If you have a taste for satirical wit, you'll probably mesh well with fans of absurdist (a.k.a. nonsensical) humor, and vice versa.

THE TREE HOROSCOPE

We all know about Capricorns, Leos, Geminis, and other familiar signs of the zodiac. But do you know about the Tree Horoscope? This version of astrology ignores the stars in the heavens and instead concentrates on earthbound flora. The system utilizes unconventional birthday groupings, but is quite illuminating in its own deep-rooted way.

Which tree is he? To divine this answer, all you need to know is the month and day of his birth.

Apple Tree

December 23 to January 1;
June 25 to July 4

This individual is likely to have a slight build and possess lots of charm. Appealing and attractive, with a pleasant aura, the Apple Tree man is flirtatious, adventurous, and sensitive, and wants to love and be loved. Although he is a carefree philosopher who lives for today, he can prove to be a faithful, tender, and generous partner.

Fir Tree

January 2 to January 11;
July 5 to July 14

Extraordinary taste, dignity, cultivated airs, and a love of beauty are hallmarks of this sign. The Fir Tree type is ambitious and talented, and might be modest, moody, stubborn, or all three. He tends to have many friends and many foes. Underneath it all, the Fir cares deeply about close friends, family, and loved ones.

Elm Tree

January 12 to January 24;
July 15 to July 25

On good days, Elm Tree men are honest and faithful partners who are noble-minded, generous, practical, stylish, humorous — and, by the way, quite attractive in the physique department. On bad days, these same wonderful ones can be unforgiving, bossy know-it-alls.

Cypress Tree

January 25 to February 3;
July 26 to August 4

The Cypress type is strong of body and flexible of mind, willing to take what life has to give and be content. This guy hates to be isolated or lonely, and looks to wealth and acknowledgment for satisfaction. He is a passionate lover and, although doggedly faithful, may be quick-tempered and may not be easily satisfied.

Poplar Tree

February 4 to February 8;
May 1 to May 14;
August 5 to August 13

Poplars make it their business to look great, but they lack confidence and need lots of support and pleasant surroundings to do their best. They can be choosy, or even critical; artistic and philosophical; organized and reliable. But no matter what their specific quirks, they take partnerships seriously.

Cedar Tree

February 9 to February 18;
August 14 to August 23

Cedars are handsome, self-confident, and healthy. They enjoy luxury but know how to adapt. These types are talented, optimistic, industrious, and determined; unfortunately, they tend to look down on others and can be impatient. The Cedar waits for his one true love but moves quickly when he knows it's right.

Pine Tree

February 19 to February 29;
August 24 to September 2

The robust Pine Tree loves agreeable company and knows how to make life comfortable. Active and natural, he is a good companion and is usually trustworthy and practical. When it comes to intimate relationships, the Pine is prone to fall in love too easily, then burn out or give up on the romance too quickly.

Weeping Willow Tree

March 1 to March 10;
September 3 to September 12

Attractive but melancholy, the Willow is a restless, capricious dreamer who desires things of beauty and may travel the world to find them. Though empathic and honest, with razor-sharp intuition, this type tends to suffer at the hand of love unless he can find a partner who provides a strong, steady anchor.

Lime Tree

March 11 to March 20;
September 13 to September 22

The Lime Tree man quietly accepts what life dishes out. Why? Because he doesn't like fussing and fighting. In extreme cases, he also resists hard work and the stress that comes with it, and so might let natural talents and bright ideas go to waste. Among friends, the Lime is loyal and sacrificing, but in love he tends to be passive, complaining, or jealous.

Oak Tree

March 21

Unusually strong and courageous, the Oak is the superhero of tree types. Unrelenting, independent, and sensible, this individual has his feet firmly on the ground, yet jumps into action whenever duty — romantic or otherwise — sounds the call.

Hazelnut Tree

March 22 to March 31;
September 24 to October 3

As a fighter for social causes, the Hazelnut man is focused, active, understanding, and dedicated. In the social realm, this sign is charming, popular, and able to make a positive and lasting impression. In the arena of love, he is generally honest and tolerant, but might have a dangerously carefree streak.

Rowan Tree

April 1 to April 10;
October 4 to October 13

The Rowan Tree type is bursting with charm and cheer, and has a love of life, art, and action. As a partner, he is both dependent and independent, offering plenty of emotional input, good company, and passion. Be sweet to Rowans; forgiveness does not come easily to them.

Maple Tree

April 11 to April 20;
October 14 to October 23

This strange and wonderful creature is shy and reserved, yet full of imagination and originality. A bit on the nervous side, he tends to have a good memory and, although reserved in public, possesses plenty of ambition and self-respect. If you want to please a Maple fellow, offer him new experiences, and prepare yourself for a bumpy ride.

Walnut Tree

April 21 to April 30;
October 24 to November 11

Not always liked, but often admired—this is the fate of those born under the Walnut Tree. Why? Because they're unrelenting, aggressive, noble, spontaneous, ambitious, ingenious, and uncommon. When it comes to love, these hardheads can be difficult, jealous, and wildly passionate.

Chestnut Tree

May 15 to May 24;
November 12 to November 21

Chestnut men are not interested in impressing others. Although they're often diplomatic, energetic, and gorgeous, they tend to feel misunderstood by the public at large, which can lead to overly sensitive or irritable behavior. Those born under the sign of the Chestnut may have trouble finding a partner, but once they do, they mate for life.

Ash Tree

May 25 to June 3;
November 22 to December 1

The ambitious, intelligent Ash does not care for criticism. Uncommonly attractive, talented, vivacious, and impulsive, this type likes to play with fate on his own terms. In the realm of romance, Ash Trees can be totally dedicated and faithful, although they sometimes let their brains rule their hearts.

Hornbeam Tree

June 4 to June 13;
December 2 to December 11

Looks are important to Hornbeam gents. They take care of their bodies, cultivate their tastes, and make their lives as comfortable as possible. Professionally, Mr. Hornbeam is reasonable and disciplined; emotionally, he often feels unsure, yet forges ahead in the search for a kind, supportive, and trustworthy partner.

Fig Tree

June 14 to June 23;
December 12 to December 21

This sign loves family, children, and animals. Though basically strong and independent, he is a bit of a social butterfly who finds fun in laziness and laughter. In a romantic relationship, the Fig keeps the peace, and in the right union, he can be inspired to let his practical talents and intelligence shine through.

Birch Tree

June 24

Those rare males born under the sign of the Birch are calm, modest, and unpretentious. Though open and friendly, they avoid anything that is excessive or vulgar. Birch Trees are drawn to the great outdoors and crave serenity in all things, including love relations. On the downside, they may be unmotivated and lacking in passion.

Olive Tree

September 23

Happiness means warm weather, good books, and stimulating company, as far as the Olive Tree man is concerned. The man of this sign is kind and cheerful, and avoids aggression and violence. In life and in love, the special Olive is sensitive, just, and free of jealousy.

Beech Tree

December 22

Keeping fit and healthy is important to this one-of-a-kind guy. He and his Beech Tree brothers are also known for their good taste, leadership qualities, and well-planned (if cautious) career paths. P.S.: They can be splendid lifetime companions.

Gazing into the Crystal Ball

Psychology, physiology, and astrology are all fascinating. But sometimes a girl needs good old-fashioned fortune-telling to make her feel connected to her feelings and her future.

Tarot cards, rune symbols, tea leaf patterns . . . these can help you take a mystical glimpse at what your love life might look like next week, next month, next year, and beyond.

Focus. Release. Believe.

THE ABBREVIATED TAROT

Tarot cards have been around since at least the fourteenth century — and probably well before. According to some schools of thought, the tarot was originally affiliated with the Kabbalah, a Jewish mystical belief system. Once used for both games of chance and fortune-telling, tarot cards provided the inspiration for modern playing cards. Through the ages, they have held on to their job as forecasters of the future.

Today's tarot deck consists of seventy-eight pictorial cards divided into two groups: the Major Arcana cards, which symbolize twenty-two universal principals, and the Minor Arcana cards, which are grouped into four suits — Swords, Wands, Cups, and Pentacles — each of which has four royalty cards and ten numbered court cards.

In the hands of a skilled practitioner, tarot cards can weave a complex story of one's past, present, and future. Traditional readings employ various spreads, in which the cards are cut, turned, and arranged in patterns that correspond to certain aspects of one's life.

It's all very interesting. But right now, you're not interested in cracking Miss Cleo's secret code. You have a far more urgent need for information and insight about that certain male who's been haunting your dreams.

I understand. That's why I'm offering a quick-and-easy numbers game that taps into the power of the tarot but doesn't require the use of an actual deck. This mini-reading references the Minor Arcana only because I think they're the most romantic and specific of the tarot cards.

All you have to do is concentrate on a subject, a

person, or a question. Follow the instructions below, then let your intuition do the rest.

STEP ONE: Choose seven numbers from 1 to 56. Write them in random order in the left-hand column of the chart below.

STEP TWO: From the numbered list that follows, locate the card that corresponds with each number you've chosen. Write its name in the appropriate space.

STEP THREE: Drawing upon the meaning of each card, make an intuitive reading that combines a card's significance with its position — that is, the indicators on the far right of the chart.

__ card: _____	= present circumstances
__ card: _____	= immediate possibilities
__ card: _____	= past actions
__ card: _____	= future actions
__ card: _____	= your potential
__ card: _____	= outside help/hindrance
__ card: _____	= outcome

THE CARDS OF THE MINOR ARCANA

Swords: The Intellect

1. King of Swords: Powerful authority figure
2. Queen of Swords: Self-sufficient, intellectual
3. Knight of Swords: Independent thinker
4. Page of Swords: A rebel with persuasive powers
5. Ten of Swords: Surrender fears
6. Nine of Swords: Anxiety brings change
7. Eight of Swords: Confusion
8. Seven of Swords: Scheming is futile
9. Six of Swords: Think logically
10. Five of Swords: Hard times, persevere
11. Four of Swords: Take a break
12. Three of Swords: Friction in friendship
13. Two of Swords: Time to reflect
14. Ace of Swords: Inspired ideas

Wands: The Spirit

15. King of Wands: Successful, philosophical
16. Queen of Wands: Charismatic, strong willed
17. Knight of Wands: Inspired, creative
18. Page of Wands: Energetic, confident, playful
19. Ten of Wands: Release energy
20. Nine of Wands: Heightened intuition
21. Eight of Wands: Breakthrough
22. Seven of Wands: Speak your mind
23. Six of Wands: Confidence, leadership
24. Five of Wands: Fight fair
25. Four of Wands: Celebrate growth
26. Three of Wands: Communicate honestly
27. Two of Wands: Focus power
28. Ace of Wands: Creative spark

Cups: Feelings and Emotions

29. King of Cups: Artistic professional
30. Queen of Cups: Sensitive, loving elder
31. Knight of Cups: A charmer
32. Page of Cups: Emotional explorer, poet
33. Ten of Cups: Emotional fulfillment
34. Nine of Cups: Wishes can be realized
35. Eight of Cups: Sadness brings growth
36. Seven of Cups: Overindulgence
37. Six of Cups: Time for personal expression
38. Five of Cups: Disappointments lead to renewal
39. Four of Cups: Express empathy
40. Three of Cups: Let's celebrate!
41. Two of Cups: Love and love
42. Ace of Cups: Happiness in love

Pentacles: The Material World

43. King of Pentacles: Successful businessman
44. Queen of Pentacles: Prosperous and generous businesswoman
45. Knight of Pentacles: Artsy-craftsy person
46. Page of Pentacles: Talented thinker
47. Ten of Pentacles: Unexpected prosperity
48. Nine of Pentacles: Working solo
49. Eight of Pentacles: Achievement through handiwork
50. Seven of Pentacles: Impatience
51. Six of Pentacles: Generosity brings success
52. Five of Pentacles: Worry and change
53. Four of Pentacles: Beware of greed
54. Three of Pentacles: Emphasize teamwork
55. Two of Pentacles: Juggle projects
56. Ace of Pentacles: Success in material matters

THE RUNES

Ahh, runes. So arcane. So enigmatic. So enlightening.

If you were absent the day they taught runes, here's a quick review: Two thousand years ago, runes were letters of an alphabet widely used by the peoples of northern Europe. They were much more than the ABC's of Norse tribes, however. Rune symbols were ascribed special powers and were used for magical inscriptions, talismans, and fortune-telling rituals. As a practical alphabet, runes fell out of favor during the Middle Ages, when Roman letterforms began to dominate Europe's written languages. But the mystical aspects of runes never faded.

Today, runic divination centers around twenty-four symbols, each of which has a meaning all its own. Advanced practitioners use runes to cast spells and enhance psychic ability; more often, however, the runes are used for readings that not only illuminate the past and the present, but suggest actions that might influence the future.

Though they have a long and convoluted history, runes are actually quite user-friendly. If you, the ardent seeker, are willing to follow some simple instructions, apply some creative energy, and call upon your intuitive powers, then you can put the runes in your pocket, so to speak. Consult them whenever you're confused or have questions—

including questions of the heart. Once you've had a bit of practice, you can give readings to other people, including the man who's got a hold on you. It's an amazing way to shed light on his secrets.

Getting Started

A proper set of runes includes 24 pieces made of stone, bone, clay, or resin, each inscribed on one side with a symbol. They are usually stored in a small cloth pouch. There's no need to run out and buy them; using the illustrations on page 196 as a guide, beginners can easily create their own set of runes.

Some options for cheap-and-easy starter kits:

- Cut 24 circular or oval shapes out of poster board and draw a symbol on each.

- Collect 24 smooth pebbles of similar size and shape, and re-create the symbols with a permanent marker.

- Find disk-shaped items of the same size and shape, such as poker chips, bingo markers, Necco Wafers, or Mentos, and use a permanent marker to draw the runes.

- Using small index cards, make your own deck of runes cards. If you choose this option, you can write each rune's meaning below its symbol.

The Runes and Their Meanings

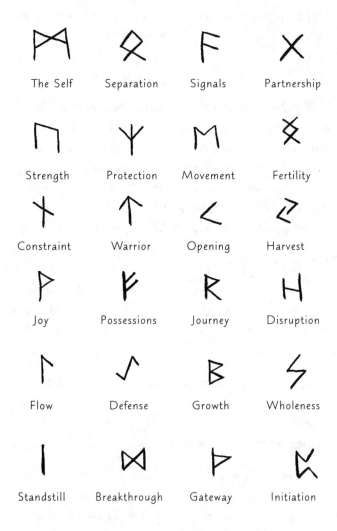

The Self	Separation	Signals	Partnership
Strength	Protection	Movement	Fertility
Constraint	Warrior	Opening	Harvest
Joy	Possessions	Journey	Disruption
Flow	Defense	Growth	Wholeness
Standstill	Breakthrough	Gateway	Initiation

A Simple Runes Reading

Like tarot cards, runes are randomly chosen, then arranged in patterns known as spreads. The simplest spread is called the Three-Rune Quickly, and it is this reading that we'll focus on. Here's how to make it happen.

1. Mix up the runes (or shuffle them, if you're using cards), while concentrating on a specific issue, situation, or problem.
2. Choose one rune and place it on a table or flat surface.
3. Choose another rune and place it to the *left* of the first one.
4. Choose a third and place it to the *left* of the second.
5. All runes should be face up. If any are face down, turn them over.
6. All symbols should be right-side up. Check the chart; if a symbol is upside down, turn it to its proper positioning.

Now you're ready to interpret the meaning of the spread.

- The rune on the far right represents the **situation as it now stands.**

- The center rune suggests the **course of action that is called for.**
- The rune on the left indicates the **end result;** that is, what will happen if you're able to meet the challenge posed by the center rune.

The more readings you do, the more you will find each rune on the chart to learn its basic meaning. Then you can draw upon your intuition and experience to make sense of the runes' wisdom.

For instance, let's say your loved one has just accepted a job that will require him to move two

Journey   Strength   Joy

states away. You focus on this difficult situation when consulting the runes, and your results are:

You can interpret this spread to mean that his pending move (Journey) is the current situation and the source of your anxiety. Your best course of action, according to the runes, is to be centered and steadfast (Strength), which will result in a happy ending (Joy).

WHAT THE TEA LEAVES REVEAL

Tea leaf reading, officially known as tasseography, has been practiced by grandmas, aunties, and other wise women for centuries. The mystical art started in China and India and has slowly migrated throughout the world.

There are many ways to interpret tea leaves, and readers from various cultures and schools of thought use different "alphabets" to divine the future. But the basic method is virtually universal: Tea is brewed, poured, and consumed. The soggy tea leaves left in the bottom of one's cup are then studied and interpreted.

It's fun to read tea leaves for yourself and your friends. Giving a reading to the man in your life is much more difficult. Why? Because your average American male thinks that drinking tea from delicate little cups is about as manly as owning a toy poodle or wearing a bow tie. Getting him to play along will require expert negotiating skills, shameless ego-stroking, and perhaps a bit of seductive reasoning. Promise to give him an in-depth reading that will foretell his future, even if you're planning to do a selfish reading and keep all the good insights to yourself.

If you can't get Mr. Wonderful to participate in

your Tea Party of Perception, don't fret. You can fill your own cup and ask the tea leaves to send messages about him.

How to Read the Leaves

1. Brew a pot of tea using loose tea — one teaspoon per cup — sprinkled in the bottom of the pot. (If you don't have any loose tea on hand, you can cut open tea bags and use those tiny little tea leaves.)

2. After three or four minutes, pour the tea into old-fashioned wide-mouth cups. Make sure each cup has a saucer.

3. Sip your tea and think about the question or issue you'd like to address. Stop drinking when there are only a few drops of tea covering the leaves in the bottom of the cup.

4. Turn the cup upside down on the saucer until all the liquid drains out. You'll be left with clumps of tea stuck to the bottom and sides of the cup; this is what you'll be reading.

The Meaning of the Leaves

Leaves at the bottom of the cup represent events that will happen one year from now; leaves at the rim of the cup indicate the present. Gauge other positionings as if the cup were a timeline. If the leaves are near the bottom, they might indicate events that will happen nine months from now; near the top, three months from now.

Look for letters, numbers, and symbols within the clumps of leaves. If you're using tea bag leaves, which are very small, you may have to play connect-the-dots to find an image.

When making your interpretation, pay attention to groupings. For instance, a horseshoe shape next to a number might mean that it's your lucky number or lucky day; a heart next to a letter suggests a romantic connection with a person who bears that initial.

Some common symbols:

> **ANCHOR:** success and stability
>
> **ARROW:** pointing up means yes; sideways means maybe; down means no
>
> **BELL:** good news
>
> **BIRD:** good luck
>
> **BOX:** surprise

CAR: travel

CIRCLE: love

CLOVER: good fortune

CROSS: unexpected bad news

CROWN: reward

FLOWER: joy

HAND: new friend

HEART: love and romance

HORSESHOE: good luck

HOUSE: happiness at home

LADDER: achievement

OVAL: new ideas bring success

QUESTION MARK: expect changes

SPIRAL: study and research pay off

STAIRS: a positive change is on the horizon

STAR: a dream will come true

SUN: happiness

TRIANGLE: unexpected events

WAXING ROMANTIC

You say you hate tea and drink only from mugs? Try a wax candle reading. This is a mystical fortune-telling practice that's quite similar in spirit to tea leaf readings, but with absolutely no caffeine. You can conduct readings for yourself and anyone you care about. Here's the good news: Guys love this exercise. Especially since it's most effective when practiced at the stroke of midnight.

Note: You don't have to stay up until midnight to do this reading, but it must be done after dark and as close to midnight as possible.

1. Fill a favorite bowl halfway with warm water.

2. Light a red candle, which is the proper color for a reading about love. Cheap candles are preferred, because they're drippier.

3. Hold the candle over the center of the bowl and let it drip until the wax begins to pile up on itself.

4. Read the meaning of the resulting shapes based on the tea leaf symbols guide (pp. 201–2) and your intuition. Don't forget to look for numbers and letters among the images.

PROJECTED LIFE SPANS

A girl's got to think ahead. If she's toying with the idea of actually marrying a guy, she's got to put on her long-distance specs and envision her life as it might appear 20, 40, or 60 years from now. There are questions of romance, real estate, and babies; famine, war, and plague; fame, trophy wives, and IRS audits; and thousands of other variables that are devilishly difficult to predict.

Thanks to the Internet, there is one x factor for which a woman can get a free and semiaccurate estimate: how long she'll live versus how long her possible future husband will live.

This is important information, though a bit gruesome, and there are plenty of Web sites that will do the math for you. Log on to any one of them (our favorite is www.hksrch.com) and fill out a brief questionnaire. You will instantly receive a scientific prediction of when you might become a widow or he might become a widower.

Here are a few examples: The subject is a male under the age of thirty who lives in the United States in a town or city with a population that's less than 2,000,000 but more than 10,000. At least one of his grandparents lived to be 85 or older. He has a graduate degree and works at a desk job for which he earns more than $80,000 per year. He isn't overweight; exercises two times per week on average; and eats like a normal human. He doesn't live alone, doesn't oversleep, drinks a bit, doesn't smoke, and considers himself to be an all-around happy guy with an easygoing attitude.

If all goes well, this man will live to be 81.

That's a ripe old age, but consider this: A woman with the exact same profile will likely be blowing out candles at her 88th birthday party.

What's even more unfair, depending on your perspective, is that a 40- to 50-year-old woman who is ten to 30 pounds overweight, earns less than $80,000 per year, smokes half a pack of cigarettes a day, and is generally unhappy is also predicted to live to the age of 88.

Men don't last as long as women. It's a fact. Don't get all sad about it, though. At least not yet. Go online, fill in the blanks, and get fascinated with far-off statistics.

M.A.S.H.

Okay, this is a pajama party game. It's not exactly imbued with mystical power, but it's lots of fun to play with a girlfriend or two, even if you're over 14.

Instructions

Draw a box and write M.A.S.H. across the top. On the left side of the box, write the names of four men you're attracted to. On the right side of the box, list four numbers from one to ten. At the bottom of the box, write down four locations or locales (towns, cities, countries, etc.).

Ask a friend to start drawing a spiral in the center of the box, until you say stop. Count the number of lines or layers in the spiral — that is your secret number.

Starting at the *M*, count the items written around the box, and cross off each item on which your number lands. Keep going until only one item is left in each category.

Key

The last man standing is the one you'll marry; the number is how many kids you'll have; the locale is where you'll live; and the letter left from M.A.S.H. is what kind of home you'll have: mansion, apartment, shack, or house.

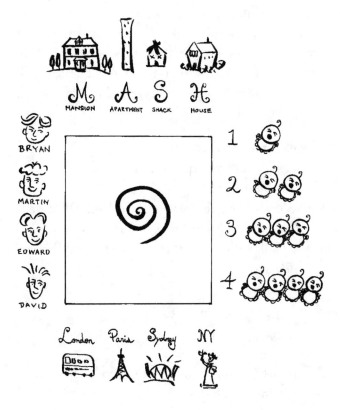

BIBLIOMANIA

This free-form fortune-telling game combines words of wisdom with random chance. It's ever so simple, but often rewards players with profound insights. Whether you try it on your own, with friends, or with your current heartthrob, bibliomania can be enlightening and inspiring.

First, you'll need books. Trashy paperbacks and dog-eared textbooks won't cut it. What you need are books that offer proverbs, pithy statements, spiritual teachings, sage observations, and the like. Search your shelves or your local library for:

- books of quotations
- books of humorous quotations
- poetry anthologies
- selections from the teachings of spiritual leaders, such as Confucius or Krishnamurti
- any book with a title that starts with *The Wit and Wisdom of* . . .

How to Play

1. Choose one book per session.

2. If you're playing with three or more people, sit on the floor in a circle.

3. Taking turns, each player holds the book and focuses on an issue, situation, or question, which can be stated out loud or kept private.

4. Next, the player ruffles the pages three times: front to back, back to front, then front to back again. On that third pass, the player stops whenever it feels right, then inserts a finger as a marker.

5. With eyes closed, the player opens the book to the chosen page and points to a place on the page.

6. The player reads the selection out loud, and the group offers comments and interpretations.

7. Follow these same rules for games that are played solo or as a duet.

With time, you'll get to know which of your books work best for bibliomania, and you'll automatically reach for them whenever you or your best guy need a little help navigating through the choppy waters of romance. When you open a book, you open your mind to new directions, insights, and perspectives.

Is It Love?

Here it is, the last chapter. The reality check. The short series of quizzes and exercises that remind you, oh romantic one, that love is sometimes an illusion caused by hormones and passionate imagination.

My advice? Read it. Learn stuff. Then follow your heart.

IS HE MR. RIGHT . . . OR MR. RIGHT NOW?

Sometimes, when a girl is swept up in a cyclone of emotions and hormones, she can fall into a state of temporary insanity and believe that the man in her life is "the one," even if he's totally inappropriate. Here's a quick reality check that will help keep those butterflies of love from clouding your vision.

For the purposes of this test, we'll call the man of your affections Bob. Answer the following questions based on the reaction you think Bob would be most likely to have.

1. After an afternoon of cross-country skiing with Bob, you go to a pub to have a bite to eat. There, Bob spots a bunch of his friends at the bar. What does he do?

__ a. He finishes eating with you, then brings you to the bar and introduces you to the gang. You all have a drink together, then he takes you home.

__ b. He invites the whole crew to join you at your table and turns your party of two into a party of eight — without consulting you first.

__ c. He finishes his meal with you, drives you home, and drops you off, then returns to the bar to hang out with his buds — without ever introducing you around.

2. You and Bob have tickets to a concert. The day before the show, you come down with the flu and have to cancel. How does he handle it?

__ a. He gives the tickets away and shows up at your door with soup and a movie.

__ b. He takes a friend to the concert, then calls you on his cell phone during the show so you can hear your favorite song.

__ c. He invites another girl to the show who is allegedly just a friend, even though you've never heard her name before.

3. You and Bob have a special date, during which he's been very sweet and generous. He wants to spend the night afterward, but you're feeling exhausted and need to be alone. How does he respond?

___ a. He swallows his disappointment and gives you your space.

___ b. He wheedles, cajoles, and tries for a good 20 minutes to talk you into it before finally giving up.

___ c. He gets angry and confrontational, and questions the future of your relationship.

4. Bob has a son who stays with him two weekends a month. One of these father/son Saturdays happens to fall on your birthday. What does he do about it?

___ a. He rearranges his schedule so that he can take you away for a romantic birthday weekend.

___ b. He plans a fun day for the three of you, including a ball game and in-line skating in the park, followed by birthday cake at his place.

___ c. He calls you on Friday to wish you a happy birthday and says he'll do something with you the following week.

5. One evening, you and Bob start discussing your past relationships. He confesses that:

__ a. He's had only a few long-term girlfriends in the past, and they broke up on good terms.

__ b. He's had lots of girlfriends in the past, but none of his relationships lasted longer than five months.

__ c. He's had relationships with both men and women, and he isn't sure which he likes better.

6. Bob loses his job. He:

__ a. Doesn't tell you about it until he's found another job, three days later.

__ b. Goes through various phases of anger, denial, and acceptance for about a week, then picks himself up and starts looking for a new job.

__ c. Asks if he can stay with you for a while so he can take some time off and get his head together.

7. You show up for a date in a brand-new pair of sexy high heels. Problem is, they make you about an inch taller than Bob. How does he respond?

__ a. He compliments you, and doesn't say a word about the height issue.

__ b. He immediately wants to bed you — and asks you to keep the shoes on.

__ c. He complains about the height problem and asks you to go home and change before he takes you out.

8. You're at a dinner party with one of Bob's former college professors, and everyone at the table is discussing a classic work of literature that you've never read. What does Bob do?

__ a. He covers for you by quickly "reminding" you of who wrote the book and what it's about.

__ b. He does nothing. He just keeps up with the conversation until the subject naturally shifts.

__ c. He notices that you're quiet and asks you, in front of everybody, if you've read the book.

Answer Key

• *A* answers belong to a man who is a true gentleman with a good heart and a kind soul. When mixed with a healthy dose of *b* answers, the guy's a good candidate for a long-term relationship. More than six *a* answers could indicate that he's a bit of a wimp. Eight *a* answers might point to a guy who is sweet to a fault, with possible clingy tendencies. Unless he's hilarious, a genius, or a great lover, a straight-*a* man might bore you into oblivion.

• *B* answers are those of a "real boy." He may not be perfect, but he isn't too good to be true. When four, five, or six *b* answers are mixed with *a* answers, you've got yourself a keeper. Seven or eight *b* answers point to a guy who might have imperfect manners or a bit too much testosterone, but there's nothing dreadful or disastrous here. He might be Mr. Right Now, but that's all right.

- C answers are all bad—and some are worse than others. Ideally, your man shouldn't have even one *c* answer on his tally (especially if it's in response to question number 5). If two or more C answers suit him, then run, run like the wind. He's Mr. Never.

TRUE LOVE ACCORDING TO SCIENTISTS

Human courtship isn't all that different from animal courtship. The flirtation that goes on in your average cocktail lounge on a Saturday night could make for a series on the Animal Planet channel. The women toss their heads, arch their eyebrows, moisten their lips, gaze with wide eyes, and look away. The men puff up their chests and square their shoulders, making their upper bodies seem as large as possible. We might as well be pumas or ostriches.

Even as we're strutting and fluffing our hairdos, we're emitting substances known as pheromones, which attract members of the opposite sex. We receive these chemical signals through our noses—yes, we literally sniff out appropriate mates—but because pheromones are odorless, we don't have a clue as to what's getting us so hot and bothered. (Sea urchins don't have a clue either, but that doesn't stop them from releasing pheromones into the water, which triggers other urchins in the colony to eject their sex cells.)

Eye contact is another important part of human courtship. When men and women look directly into each other's eyes, one of two responses is triggered: advance or retreat. The advance response is accompanied by the dilating of the pupils and, more often than not, the stretching of the mouth into something we call a smile. The most flirtatious of the 18 different smiles we're capable of is the "open smile," which exposes both the top and the bottom row of teeth.

There are five distinct phases of flirting. Here's how they might play out at a dance party:

1. Both men and women stake out a territory from which they can observe and be observed, such as a table to sit at or a wall to lean against. From there, they draw attention to themselves by posing attractively, batting their eyes, laughing, being animated, etc.

2. The recognition stage comes next. This is when two people acknowledge each other through eye contact and, perhaps, smiling. If all goes well, they

move closer to one another so that they're within talking range.

3. Conversation begins. This starts with simple exchanges such as compliments, witty remarks, or the ever-popular "Wanna dance?" These small but important exchanges are known by anthropologists as "grooming talk" and may go on for some time, leading to exchanges of phone numbers or plans to meet again.

4. Now it's time for touch. This phase begins with "intention cues," where one or both parties move closer together until one touches the other. A hand on a knee, an arm around a shoulder, a slow dance . . . this is fairly innocent stuff, but it is loaded with meaning and is often sexually super-charged. At this point, it's important that the person being touched signals that the advances are welcome. Otherwise, all hopes of further court-ship come to an abrupt halt.

5. The final stage of flirting is when two people start mirroring each other's moves. They sit or stand face-to-face, they look into each other's eyes, their limbs synchronize — in other words, they get their groove thang on (although scientists might not put it quite that way).

Advanced courtship is just as animalistic as the early phases. For instance, in a recent study of 1,000 unmarried American males, 63 percent reported that they'd had inaugural intercourse with a new girlfriend after a dinner date, as opposed to the 32 percent who scored after a drinks date. Why is this significant? Because by taking a woman to dinner and paying for her meal, a man demonstrates that he is a good hunter and provider. This makes the female feel like she's making a good mating choice and prompts one thing to lead to another.

Feelings of love and infatuation are products of our personal chemistry sets. Emotionally, we go through three love phases:

1. The person we're attracted to takes on a new level of significance or special meaning to us.

2. We start to have intrusive thoughts about our object of affection, leading to much daydreaming involving wild, romantic scenarios or the mental replaying of certain shared moments.

3. We crystallize our feelings about that person. This means that we notice his weaknesses or flaws, but instead of rejecting them, we consider them cute or part of a whole desirable package.

Chemically, the feeling of being in love — including elation, exhilaration, and euphoria — is caused by molecules known as phenylethylamines (PEA) that stimulate neurons in the limbic system. The bad news is that the human brain can only endure high levels of PEA for about one to three years. Then — assuming the relationship can survive the shift — one's inner chemical wizard trades PEA for endorphins, which produce a general feeling of well-being. Thus, the love affair slowly shifts from being tremendously exciting to feeling pleasant and comfortable. Sort of like a girl and her trusty dog. *Sigh*. Animal Planet all over again.

Secret note: Have you ever quietly initiated a relationship, then let the man feel as though he made it happen? You're not alone. In the United States, it's been shown that a woman generally gets the courtship dance started, using subtle clues that are usually nonverbal. Then she allows what's called an "initiative transfer," in which the man picks up on her lead and moves in — and believes all along that he's the one who started the flirtation.

TRUE LOVE ACCORDING TO LOVERS

Do you have trouble identifying your feelings or putting them into words? Don't feel inadequate; millions of people have the same frustration. Love is as individual as fingerprints, faces, the patterns in a cluster of tea leaves, and the wild fantasies that make you stay awake at night, scribbling in your journal, staring at the ceiling, and wondering what's to become of you. Emotions can be so overwhelming that mere words seem feeble — unless, of course, those words were penned by masters of language.

Take a look at the following sentiments. Read them out loud. Then choose one or two quotations that sound like they've come straight from your heart, and read the explanation.

1. "Love opens the doors into everything as far as I can see, including and perhaps most of all, the door into one's own secret and often terrible and frightening, real self."

— *May Sarton*

2. "If only one could tell true love from false love as one can tell mushrooms from toadstools."

— *Katherine Mansfield*

3. "Love is a fire. But whether it is going to warm your heart or burn down your house, you can never tell."

— *Joan Crawford*

4. "There is no surprise more magical than the surprise of being loved: It is God's finger on man's shoulder."

— *Charles Morgan*

5. "One word frees us of all the pain and weight of life: That word is love."

— *Sophocles*

6. "To love is to receive a glimpse of heaven."

— *Karen Sunde*

7. "I want to love first, and live incidentally."

— *Zelda Fitzgerald*

8. "It's not the men in my life that count, it's the life in my men."

— *Mae West*

9. "One should always be in love. That is the reason one should never marry."

— *Oscar Wilde*

10. "When two people love each other, they don't look at each other, they look in the same direction."

— *Ginger Rogers*

11. "A successful marriage requires falling in love many times, always with the same person."

— *Mignon McLaughlin*

12. "Look for a sweet person. Forget rich."

— *Estée Lauder*

13. "An archaeologist is the best husband a woman can have; the older she gets, the more interested he is in her."

— *Agatha Christie*

14. "Anyone who's a great kisser, I'm always interested in."

— *Cher*

15. "If love is the answer, could you please rephrase the question?"

— *Lily Tomlin*

1–3: *The Tentative Romantic*

You're scared, but your emotions are stirred. Go forth and have the romantic adventure of your life. Whether it lasts forever or disintegrates upon contact, remember: This is the way of love.

4–6: *The Romantic's Romantic*

Your dream of love encompasses passion, philosophy, and redemption. Is he as deep as you? Jump in and find out. Win or lose, this is the way of love. Be brave.

7–9: *The Reckless Romantic*

Love for love's sake is your game. When pursuing your latest conquest, you might just find a reason to be the best possible you. Keep an open heart. Be honest. This is the way of love.

10–12: *The Seasoned Romantic*

You understand the profound beauty of long-term relationships and have what it takes to survive the rough spots and revel in the sweet and lasting rewards. This, again, is the way of love.

13–15: *The Realistic Romantic*

Nobody can fool you. You're a levelheaded realist and will stay grounded even while being swept off your feet. Take a few risks. Let yourself go once in awhile. This is the way of love, and it's there for you to explore with all of your heart and soul.